Fresh Read

Studying the Bible without the Hype

By Dave Paul Campbell

Copyright 2022

CONTENTS

About the Author

Dave Campbell lives near Seattle and is a seasoned minister/counselor. He traveled for many years, singing and evangelizing in the Northwest. He made several appearances on TBN's local Praise the Lord program as well as other television appearances in Alaska, Seattle, and Vancouver areas. When Dave stopped touring, he became a children's pastor and began introducing innovative techniques for bringing the Bible to life for young minds. After a miraculous touch of God at a local camp meeting, he launched "Joy of Freedom" outreach ministry and pastored it for 9 years. The outreach is still ministering to the homeless, destitute, and chemically dependent individuals, today.

Among many pastoral privileges, Dave has spent many hours counseling people with severe life issues. The experience he has gained for practical life applications of Biblical principles has been invaluable. Dave brings many things to the counseling table, including good common sense and a ground-roots approach to difficult and sensitive challenges.

Contact Information: info@davecampbellbooks.com

Website: davecampbellbooks.com

Also, find *Dave Paul Campbell* on Facebook.

Foreword

The Bible is a very big book, and it is very old. This alone is ample reason to believe that a truckload of people have read it and interpreted what it says. Since so many people have not only read it but dissected it in every imaginable way, it can be difficult for many Christians to determine the difference between accurate interpretation and just fanciful musing. There are many teachers, in thousands of churches, as well as on radio and television. Of course, most of them seem to claim their viewpoint is correct, and that everyone else's is wrong. Now, if you have been a Christian for many years, you have heard a lot of sermons and lectures, so your head is swimming in a sea of information that is sometimes conflicting. Perhaps this is one reason that many Christians have stopped reading the Bible. The more they read, the more confused they get. This is tragic because it cuts off an important life-line to Spiritual food that we desperately need. My question is this: How do we get to a place where we are more comfortable reading the Word? And, how do we easily study the Word a little deeper, so there is a richer and more accurate way of getting what the author was trying to convey? The answer to that is in this book. Dave has set out a simple path that allows you to see God's Word more purely. The idea is to set aside all the things that have been imposed on scripture and extract just what the writer put down on the Bible page. To aid in this process, Dave has introduced a set of just 3 rules for reading the Bible. These can help bring out the truth while weeding out fanciful theories. Come along with Dave on this study journey and see how clear the Bible can truly be.

Chapter 1

Bad Bible Study?

Is there such a thing as "bad Bible study?" Hmm. I'm not sure this is true. Perhaps as long as the study is consistent and persistent, it is "good." Where it seems to veer off into "la la land," is when short passages are combined to create doctrines that are not clearly stated on a single page. I'll give you one classic example:

Matthew 27:5 "… Judas threw the money into the temple and left. Then he went away and hanged himself."

Luke 10:37 "... Jesus told him, "Go and do likewise."

Can you see the problem here? Unfortunately, many scholars have similarly created scriptural nightmares. Verses that sound like they could be about the same subject matter are connected, and yet the scriptures used do not indicate they should be connected. Thus, the connection is somewhat arbitrary. As an example, here is a question: Are all verses that mention trumpets talking about the same thing? Are they all talking about the same trumpet or the same events? Hmm.

I think it is time we put some traditions and traditional interpretations of the Bible on the shelf for a day and see what the Bible says – and what it does not say. If this sounds like a kind of soapbox preaching, I apologize, but the point is valid. We desperately need to know the truth. We need to clear the smoke of all the opinions, conjectures, and theories. We need to purify our faith and our doctrine. What stands the test of scrutiny (test by fire) is what we should firmly hold onto. What is not clearly scriptural, we should discard, and what is questionable should be shelved until we can prove it right or wrong. What do I mean by "shelved?" I mean, to not teach it as fact or share it with others as doctrine.

The further I walk in this life, the more I am convinced that deep love for God, drives us to know what he has said. Not so much what man has said about what God said, but what God actually said, in its purest form. I want to remove as many middle men as possible and weed out what is "fill in" and "add on." I do not want other people filling in between the lines of the Bible. I want just the Bible. Similar to a method R.C. Sproul has notably forwarded: Let the Bible explain itself.

Story

When I was a young adult, there was a time when I needed to buy a propane torch. I do not remember why, but it likely was to thaw some pipes or break loose some rusty parts. As young men do – okay, older men do too – I "played" with the torch. I suppose it is a little like getting a new car and wanting to find out how fast it can go. Since I had not owned one before, I wanted to find out what it could do, so I tried applying the high heat to different things, to see the effect. Rocks were not phased much; maybe blackened some. Occasionally, parts of a rock would pop off, but mostly they were just boring. Wood burned, of course – duh, but when I turned my torch on steel metals, they didn't do anything but get red hot. They didn't even seem to bend any easier. Then I pointed my torch close to a soda pop can. It did not take long before parts of it melted. It was almost delightful to see how quickly the metal dissolved into a tiny molten lake. I think the most surprising takeaway that day was how little aluminum is used to make a can!

Is there a moral to this story? Well of course. After all, why else talk about a dumb aluminum can? I mean, this book is not about methods of recycling, right? The point here is that when certain things are put under high heat, they melt away and look nothing like they were before. We tend to see their true nature. God has done this with many people and he does it with us. We are all put through the fire of testing to see if what we say is actually what we believe. The tests prove that what our mouth proclaims is actually in our hearts. God tests and proves the quality of our character. He desires to see our ultimate trust in him and his incredible love. Similarly, we are instructed by God's Word to test and prove what we are told, dig into scripture, and be sure of what we believe. It is not enough to just parrot what we were told. Let's also remember that Jesus was the only perfect teacher. Men are flawed and can be influenced by all kinds of things – even eating tainted food.

So, what we were taught is a good launching point, but each one of us, must go from there and work out our beliefs and our salvation. I do not at all mean to throw out everything we believe. Some have done that and shipwrecked their faith. What I mean is to take a close look at each part of what we believe, one at a time, while holding onto everything else. If what we believe is true, it will stand firm. If it is shaky, then we need further evaluation. In the end, we may need to discard some things completely.

GIGO

Many people know of the term "GIGO." I think it is a result of computer programming, but it stands for "garbage in, garbage out." When programming, if the code is corrupt, the computer's output will be corrupt. This concept was used in illustrations, motivational talks, and sermons for years. I hate to even mention it, because of the over-use. So, why do I feel the need to bring in this concept? Because it exactly matches some methods of Bible study. In many church Bible studies, the process of learning is backward. Someone (or a group of people) decides what they are going to teach about a passage of scripture, then they prepare questions or comments that lead students in a specific direction of thought. It is all planned out so it "spoon feeds" the student. They don't have to think, they just have to remember. Year after year, we spoon-feed a certain way of thinking and expect people to remember that thinking. Year after year, the student sits and takes it all in. Eventually, they can recite everything they were indoctrinated with and firmly believe they "know the Bible." Do they - or do they only know the commentary of their mentor?

The biggest problem is that when the student can replay what they were shown, then they are considered to be qualified to teach. So, what do they teach? Exactly what they were told. They firmly and staunchly hold onto what they were told, without checking anything out themselves. And, what happens when they are asked a hard question or asked to defend their view? Their learning is shallow, so they don't truly know why they believe the way they do. It is not necessarily that they believe wrongly, they just do not have a solid foundation. There is no "why" behind the belief. There is no person (Christ) driving their belief. It is just a set of rules and principles. This is not true faith. It is more like membership in a club. Just say all the right things and play by the rules and everything will be fine. Can I get a buzzer about now?

Jesus is our focus, our trust, our hope, our friend, and our teacher. Our deep relationship with him drives us to see and learn more. Thus, we dig into scripture more, because there we see a reflection of all that he is. We come to know him better and more intimately. This close relationship with Christ is the end-all; not a creed or creative poetry, but his Word, spoken directly to our heart, proving over and over, just how much he loves us.

A Word about Being Protestant

When it comes to digging into the Word ourselves and learning on our own, I cannot leave out one of the most important historical aspects. Before Martin Luther was born, the Christian church was called "catholic." It is a generic term that means universal or all-embracing. This had significant meaning when Christianity was declared the state religion in the third century. The language in the Roman Empire was and had been Latin. Latin was considered by many to be the "perfect" language. Even today, many see the value of how exact the meanings were in Latin words and phrases. So, the Bible was translated into Latin. The Old Testament had been written in Hebrew-Aramaic and the New Testament was predominantly in Greek. Now, in the Roman Empire, the business language was Greek. This is why the New Testament was in Greek, so people of different natural languages could read it. Why the Catholic Church did not translate the Bible all into Greek I am not sure. The Jews had already done that with the Old Testament before Jesus was born (see the Septuagint). Regardless of the reasons, the Catholic Church used the Latin version in their services (Mass). Of course, over time, many people did not know Latin, so it was the obligation of the priests to teach the Bible. Since no one had individual copies of the Bible (nor did the Jews have individual copies of the Old Testament), everyone had to hear the Bible and learn what it said, at the church. Over time, the ideas in the Bible were tailored to match Catholic doctrine. The general idea in church leadership at the time of Martin Luther was that people would not understand the Bible if they read it themselves. Of course, as many know, Martin Luther saw a huge flaw in that policy. He believed the common pew-sitter had a right to read the Word for themselves. He saw God's Spirit as a guiding force to the truth, not just the priest. As printing technology advanced, the possibility of people having access to the Bible became more possible and with the printing press, other translations began to emerge. In a decade or two, Martin Luther's goals began to gain real ground. The Bible could be offered in German and even in English (see Tyndale). More and more the scriptures were opened up. It seemed this fanned the flames of the protestors (Protestants) and more people chose to break away from the Catholic Church, seeing that their doctrines contradicted what the Bible actually said.

Based on this history and our fight, as Protestants, to keep the scripture open for all to read, I have to ask a question: Why are Protestants not exercising a right that was bought with the blood of many people? Men were persecuted and some were even killed when they separated from the Catholic Church. And when Tyndale translated it into English they were outraged and people burned him alive.

We have a grave responsibility to read our easily obtained Bibles. We need to keep in step with our founding faith-fathers and absorb this wonderful gift we have been given. In it are the very Words of Life. We do not have to just listen to someone who says they are teaching the Bible correctly. We can check out what we are hearing. We can do as Martin Luther did: Look into the Bible ourselves and be fed from it, on our own. With the help of the Holy Spirit, we can learn incredible things. Things we have not seen before or understood before. And all this can be from just simply reading what is on the page.

"GIGO" is not what we want when it comes to Bible Study. If we take garbage ideas into our study, we will come out with garbage ideas. In fact, if we take ANYTHING into God's Word, we are in error, before we read the first line. God's Word was given to us to read. We take in that Word and we learn from it – every time we read it. If we read a word, phrase, or paragraph, and immediately say, "Oh, I know what this is. I have heard this taught," then we cannot learn. When we think we have it all figured out, we stop learning. We must not take ideas into our Bible reading. We must extract what God has placed there.

We do not plant things into God's Word, we harvest what he planted there for us.

Yes, when you become mature in Christ, there will be times when you remember other scriptures that dovetail into what you are reading and it is okay to even go and look at those verses. But, those connections should never completely overshadow what you are currently reading. They are good support, but should not be the main event in your reading.

How Do We Deal with All This?

So, what do we do? How do we avoid the pitfalls of taking our pet doctrines into the Bible when we read? How do we see the new things God wants to show us? Well, frankly it is a challenge and I would say that it takes practice. I also think that we need some help getting there. This book is designed to be exactly that. I want to help get you to that first giant step. I want to help you be able to see more clearly what God's Word says and does not say. What I do not want to do is teach you doctrine - and I do not want this book to be a commentary on Biblical text. Yes, I will throw in some things that I have found and tell you what my impressions are on a specific text (as an example), but as always in my series of books, I leave most of the conclusions to you. My goal is to show you how to study in a new and fresh way, and how to avoid getting bogged down in theoretical doctrines and doomsday philosophies. You can even apply what you learn to end-times studies and find much more truth than before. By laying aside what "might be," and sticking with just what was written, you will start to see the heart of the writer, rather than your mental creations.

The Who is Very Important

Before we move on and explore actual study methods (in the next chapter), I want to talk briefly about an area where many scholars make errors. When reading the Bible, we must always take into account to who the text is written. As much as we might want the entire Bible to be a personal letter to us, it is not. It is God, relaying his will and plan, through the pen of a man. Each book of the Bible was written for a specific purpose and written with the idea that a certain set of people should read it. Now, this does not mean that God excludes us. We are supposed to read it and glean what God has said, but not in the context that all the things said were specifically directed to us. If we act like everything is specific to us, then we best get marching through seas, sacrificing animals, and marching around Jericho. Instead, we need to see what God said to those he loved and cared for. We learn God's character and we learn countless lessons about what to do and what not to do as Christians. We learn about how the Messiah was foretold, and how he came. We learn what the early church struggled with and see that it was much the same as what we struggle with today. We learn from what Godly men instructed those churches to do – and how they should live. Many things in God's Word can be applied to our Christian walk, today. These things seem to emerge as obvious, and with the leading of the Holy Spirit, we then know how to live our lives and walk right with Christ. If we know why Jesus needed to come and die for us; we know how to accept his salvation plan; and we know how to live the way Jesus wants us to, this is the core of what the Bible teaches. We could say that the rest of the Bible is largely examples that support these basics. So, every time you read, remember who the book was originally written by, and remember who he was writing it to or for (at that time).

Chapter 2

Fresh Read

Imagine for a few minutes that you were fighting in the Second World War. The branch of the military you were assigned to was the Navy and you were selected to serve aboard a submarine. For long periods, you breathed stale, recirculated air. All the odors of the submarine were also circulated. So you are in a pretty tight space, with the body odors of many other men, who may not smell all that nice. Yes, you do your job, try not to complain too much, and tolerate the consistently uncomfortable circumstances – but oh, when you can surface and open that hatch, wow. There is nothing like that breath of fresh air.

When studying the Bible, it is easy to get bogged down with the "usual." When we discuss doctrines with others, we hear the same stale reasoning and begin to wonder if anyone truly believes all that they are mechanically reciting. And, when it comes to end-times studies (Eschatology), the air gets thick, very quick. Okay, that is not good English, but then I needed to make it rhyme. ☺ But, in all seriousness, do you find it quite tedious, when so many people have their own theories about how the world is going to end? No one truly agrees about what will happen in the future, and for good reason. No one knows what is going to happen. There may or may not be glimpses of the future in the Bible, but I think all scholars can agree that we are not told about everything that will happen. So, our future is uncertain. This makes people uncomfortable and insecure. I think much of the speculation about end-times passages in the Bible comes from people simply wanting to know what their future holds. And, of course, they want it to be bright and rosy. Uncomfortable or not, the truth is that God has not revealed our exact, daily future. Regardless of what we believe, most of us, if not all, will die a natural death and be escorted into the presence of Christ. Maybe this is our real security.

Apart from the security issues, however, we need to deal with this onslaught of information and disinformation concerning God's Word. As I said, the discussions are tedious. Perhaps this has driven people out of God's Word and away from meaningful dialogue about his Word. Maybe we have made the discussions as taboo as politics. Heated debates about who is right, could have become a reason to just avoid the subject. Confusion about the Bible in general may be discouraging people from opening the cover. Perhaps memes from social media are more palatable and bring out less anger. Is there a fix for all this? Is there a way to sidestep the theological wars and come to cherish what is on the pages of our Bible? I believe so, but it does not seem to be on the same road with reciting preprogrammed responses to Biblical questions. So, where does this road start? Let me show you what I think.

When We Think We're Right

Now if you have read any of my other books in this series, most of this chapter will be a review, otherwise, please read this chapter carefully. It sets the stage for most of the content in this book.

If you have lived very long on this planet, you have likely been in a situation where you were sure you were right, then discovered you were wrong. How about the opposite? Did you hear something that made you doubt your belief, then discover you were right after all? Well, I have good news for you. You're human! Living on planet earth can be confusing and sometimes even maddening, yet we all seem to take some level of pride in being right in our beliefs - and our beliefs don't even need to be religious. For instance, you can believe with all your heart and mind that you turned off the stove, yet it can still be on. One question that rolls around in my head is this: Why is it so important for people to be right, and why do we feel so badly when we're wrong? Could it be just a simple matter of pride? Let's explore this idea as we look at a lady who made a total commitment to her belief.

The Power of Green Stuff

A lady in our family (who shall remain unnamed) went to lunch with other family members at a local buffet. She was having a good time until she put a bite of some "green stuff" in her mouth and quickly started gasping. After much water and time, she was finally able to explain her intense discomfort. Apparently, when she saw a fairly large bowl of what looked like Guacamole, she took several heaping spoonfuls and deposited them on her food. Unfortunately, the green stuff was Wasabi. Now, we can all laugh at her, and I'm pretty sure many family members did, but every one of us has been in a similar situation. We look at all the evidence and carefully deduce that certain things are facts. Once we're convinced of our facts, we act on them, wholeheartedly. Case in point, if the lady I mentioned had doubted even a little about the green substance she put on her plate, she would have tasted a tiny portion of it before committing to a large bite. The truth is that she wholeheartedly believed the green stuff was something different than it was.

The Altar of Truth

There are many views, beliefs, and interpretations of God's Word - and then there's what the writer meant. Clearing all the man-made smoke is not always easy, but some tools make the job a little easier (we'll talk about those a little later). One thing is clear to me: The most important truths in the Bible are repeated and presented in simple ways that anyone can understand. This proves to me that God is fair and just and that he wants to connect personally with each of us. Perhaps this is an indication that our first tool for clearing away all the preconceived ideas about the Bible is to simply read it like we would any other book and try to see what the actual text says, without manipulation. There's a principle that goes along with this method and it goes something like this:

If we care about what God is trying to say to us, sooner or later we will need to sacrifice our pet doctrines on the "Altar of Truth."

No matter what we believe, or have been taught, if we want to get to what matters, we need to put it all in the "fire" so it can be tested. What survives the test of truth's fire, is what you want to hold onto. What is destroyed, is what needs to be trashed anyway and what is charred needs to be re-examined with a better microscope. Does this sound like a good and sound practice? I think it is and I have proven that it works over a very long time.

Now, in all fairness, I must give credit where it is due. I am not the author of this idea about the "Altar of Truth." At one time in my life, I was trying to answer difficult questions about some scriptures in the Bible. I found that some things I had been taught didn't seem to have a very firm base in scripture. As I dug deeper, I also discovered wonderful truths about some of the things I had long believed. Along this path of discovery, however, I also discovered what I call "black holes" in traditional doctrines. It was about this same time, I heard Hank Hanegraaff (Bible Answer Man) on the radio, talking about the idea of "placing pet doctrines on the Altar of Truth." Since this was already beginning to happen in my life, I was encouraged to continue the journey. What followed was an ongoing exploration of the Bible with a new set of glasses that helped me see some awesome truths in God's Word and also see the outlines of false doctrines that had no real substance. Now, to be honest, I've not been able to find this "Altar of Truth" quote from any other source, so I can't be certain whether Hank Hanegraaff was quoting someone else or whether it was something our Lord showed him - but for this book, I want to thank him for broadcasting what I consider to be a well-said truth.

A New Dress?

Though I may be a little uncertain about where the phrase "Altar of Truth" originated, there is a quote I am sure of:

> **"Old error in new dress is ever error nonetheless."**

C.S. Lewis said this and I certainly could not have said it better. The truth is that since the time of the Apostles, there have been many heresies in the Christian community, yet there are no new ones - just the same old ones in different clothes. With so many false teachings out there, finding the real truth can be daunting. I hope that this book will help you find simple ways to read prophetic scripture. If nothing else, I hope you can at least come to see what prophetic scripture is not. You may never see all the truth in a passage when you read it, but you can certainly weed out a lot of things that are not true and take a closer look at questionable things.

Perhaps it will help you to know some of the things I do when I read the Bible: As I read, and study God's Word, there are things I see that seem to connect to other scriptures. Exploring the clear and obvious connections between what I am reading and other scriptures that are similar can help bring clarity and definition to what I am reading. One thing I will admit: After years of study, there are some scriptures where you can almost "read between the lines" of what the writer said. However, no matter how many positive suspicions or private musings I may want to share with my close Christian friends, I never teach or preach what I can't prove in scripture. One very important thing I want to share with you is this: A long time ago, I stopped just repeating what I was taught and purposed to teach only doctrine that stands on absolutely firm, provable ground. I hope after reading this book that you, too, will take up this mantle, and teach only what you can firmly prove from Biblical text.

The Rules

Rules, rules, rules! None of us like a truckload of rules, right? But, without any guidelines, we could never even find our socks! This being said, let me make a promise to you: For this study, there will be very few rules. In fact, we will use only three simple rules and you can remember them by the acronym R.I.D. (RID). I chose this acronym because, what we want to do is RID ourselves of theory, manufactured doctrines, and manipulated scripture. Here is the definition of RID:

1. Read without prejudice

2. If it's weird, compare

3. Don't play God

Now, let's see what each one of these means:

Read Without Prejudice

Imagine for a moment you are a new Christian and you've never read the Bible. Each phrase and each verse is fresh and new. You haven't spent a lifetime in church, so you don't have a thousand sermons floating around in your head. As you read, you take in each idea, like you would read any other book. Yes, you have much more respect and awe for this book because it's God's Word, but you don't automatically look for hidden meanings and you don't expect that what is said is anything more or less than what is written. In your enthusiasm, you hang on to every word - not wanting to miss anything.

Now, import this scenario into your own Bible-life. What is different? Let me suggest that you've probably heard the passage you are reading several times and heard many sermons about it. When you read it, all this stuff swims around in your head. It's hard to separate what the passage is saying from all the things you've been told about it. Your mind also wants to fill in the blanks and mold the passage into 21st-century America. So, the task here is to slow down – and I mean slow way down - and read each word like it was your first time. Instead of thinking about what you have heard, simply look at the verse and hear what it is saying. Perhaps the writer simply meant exactly what he wrote. Like in other literature, imagine that a writer in the Bible is trying to communicate a simple idea through words! Okay, maybe that was a little sarcastic and likely a bit snarky, but we can do a terrible disservice to the original manuscript and our soul when we immediately assume there is much more to a verse than what is on the page. So, when you are reading God's Word, always try to read just what is on the page, first, and try to read it like you have never seen it or heard about it before. This is what I call a "Fresh Read," and it is the basis for an entire study method. It brings us back to basics. It gives us a purer look at what the author intended. This principle is important because it is built on the idea that

God intended his Word to be understood by even an unlearned person or a person with disabilities. Thus, the most important things we can glean from the Bible are those doctrines that are main and plain. This is what we should be looking for when we read. Not fanciful manipulations of texts to produce wow factors, but the raw, undiluted Word of God. The sweet messages of love and intimacy from God's mouth to our hearts, as well as the consequences of turning away from God.

If it's Weird, Compare

Sometimes when you read a passage in the Bible, it sounds funny and is not quite clear. In these cases, just a little study, or further reading, usually clears up the confusion. However, prophecies can be different. There are often visions or dreams. In these, some images represent people, nations, and events. In some cases, God says what they mean, and in other cases, he does not. But, it is also important to see that there are instances where God has said something to a nation and it has been thoroughly taught to the people of that nation over many years (even many generations). When phrases and symbolism are embedded in culture this way, God does not have to explain what he means when he uses the same symbolic phrases again. So when we read the Bible and things sound a little weird, we need to remember that the Bible was written to other people, in another culture, at another time. So what was very clear to them, might not be as clear to us. Now, how do we resolve this issue? One way is to compare what we read with other verses in the Bible that have a similar phrasing or symbolism. If God says I am going to sound a trumpet and does not explain it, then we can look at other verses that refer to God blowing a trumpet (or God having a trumpet blown). Yes, it may take a little digging but it's not hard and it's not rocket science. Since the whole Bible is in digital format, searching for a specific phrase (even through all sixty-six books) is quick and painless. So, if a word or phrase you are reading seems weird, look for other uses. If the phrase was used in an Old Testament verse that was about judgment, then you can rightfully conclude that the author in the New Testament (who knew the Old Testament passages) is likely referring to judgment. You will be amazed how many times this approach works and you don't have to be an expert to spot the similarities. In this way, we also carry on the methods of Bible experts like R.C. Sproul, who taught that the Bible should be the best source for defining itself.

Don't Play God

For me, this is the biggest issue: People are constantly trying to figure out what they "feel" is unfulfilled prophecies Now there is little doubt that for Jesus' disciples, there are many future events that were foretold. They were warned about many things. Some of Jesus' foretelling seemed to be pretty clear to them, while others remained a mystery until they started coming to pass. But, whether Biblical text is read from their view or ours when symbols are uncertain it is bad theology to simply assign what we think. So here is the simple rule for what I consider proper prophetic study:

If God didn't say, then neither should you!

What does this phrase mean? Simply this: There are many places in prophecy where God said a symbol meant something. In some cases, a powerful animal in a vision represented a nation. In other cases, a dream of certain food meant there was going to be a famine. These were things that God told those who were involved. The prophetic words of Jesus' are not much different. In some places, Jesus explains his symbolism – at other times he does not.

Here is something important: Notice that I did not say that in the prophecy the image was the other thing. In prophecies, the real object, person, or landscape is not shown. God seems to never show a view-screen of a future world. In Revelation, for instance, Jesus shows John figures that represent people, nations, and events. So, we need to be very careful that we don't play God and try to explain things that God did not. Now for instance, if the people John was writing to understood something he wrote because of phrases they were familiar with, that's different, but in cases where there is new symbolism, we need to leave it to what God wants us to know and what he doesn't. Here is a fact we must accept:

God has never told anyone, everything about their future.

At best, God gives us a glimpse of the future and only tells us what we need to know. When we use our own ideas to fill in prophetic gaps, it is a mistake. Here is one reason why: For hundreds of years, the religious experts in Israel/Judah looked at prophecies about the Messiah (Jesus). They thought they had the whole scenario figured out. They just knew how the Messiah would come, and what he would do. In turn, they taught the people what they had deduced. How did this all turn out? Not so good. When Jesus came, he fulfilled the prophecies differently than they had envisioned and as a result, the religious leaders rejected the Messiah. Thus, many people missed the first coming of the Messiah. So it stands to reason that if scholars of any age use the same kind of conjecture with Jesus' prophetic statements, they could miss what he truly said to his disciples.

Carts and Horses

One common, but somewhat antiquated phrase is "Don't put the cart before the horse." However, in America we don't see all that many horse-drawn carts, so the imagery may be a little hazy to most people. Because it is the right concept for what I am going to propose, I would like you to stop for a minute and picture a horse in your head. Once you have that image fully detailed, then imagine a horse carriage. Now, place yourself in the scene with these two objects. You are standing there on the side of the road and in front of you is this carriage and standing behind the carriage (facing the carriage) is the horse. A person is sitting in the carriage and wants to go into town - so to accommodate them you yell to the horse, giddy up! Now, in your mind, what happens with the horse and carriage after you yell this command? Hmm. In my mind, the best-calculated actions are as follows:

1. The horse completely ignores you and nothing happens.

2. The horse bolts; runs around the carriage; and takes off down the street, leaving the carriage behind.

Now, let's alter the scenario. The horse is still behind the carriage, but you have somehow hitched the horse's neck to the back of the carriage. Now, when you yell giddy up, what does the horse do? Hmm. Well, we could hope the horse would somehow, push the carriage, but have you ever seen a horse do this? Would the horse even try? Hmm - I am thinking at best the horse may just look at you with an expression of "You have got to be kidding!" So, I think we can rightfully say, that putting the cart in front and the horse in the back, is ridiculous and just does not work in any sensible scenario.

Now, you may be starting to wonder if there is a point here besides the lesson on how to hitch up a horse. The answer is yes. One of the simple, yet most important things to remember when considering prophecies is that they come in a God-purposed order. In other words, God spoke to men about the future, when he chose to do so. When he wanted to reveal more about that same future, then he often added more details later. In some cases, the closer the time came for certain events to occur, the more details were given. This becomes critical when studying scripture because when we are trying to define the meaning of images and odd terms, it is crucial to place the weight of the meanings on the later revelations. For example, if there is some confusion about things that seem to be similar in the Book of Revelation and the Book of Daniel, then we use Revelation to define what is shown in Daniel, not the other way around. This being said, it is acceptable for the overall meaning of symbols and terms to be homogenous. The meanings may sort of flow back and forth between two or more books. However, if there is any question between books about the details of the events, we should take God's later revelation as the more detailed. Thus, the more detailed account of future events trumps the lesser detailed account. As an overarching example: What Isaiah, Ezekiel, or Daniel wrote about the future was more defined by what Jesus said to his disciples, and what Jesus said to his disciples was then even more defined by what he told/showed John on the Island of Patmos.

Connecting Verses

I have to be very honest here. One of my pet peeves is when scholars start connecting verses to build a doctrine. The main and plain doctrines are stated as a lesson in the Bible. We do not have to create them with fancy footwork. If I have to pull 10 isolated scriptures from all over the Bible, to support my beliefs, then I need to reexamine my beliefs. If a Bible writer quotes another writer (such as an Old Testament prophet), then we know the writer's ideas are connected, but if there is no reference to other texts within the writing itself, we should not assume that the writer was intending for a connection to other texts. Yes, if the principles or doctrines in each text are obvious and they obviously teach the same thing, then we are pretty safe to bring them together and use them for teaching. However, just because the same word is used in two texts, does not demand that they are talking about the same thing. So, my friend, be very careful how you read and how your cross reference texts. And, be very wary of Bible teachers who form theories that are based on connecting many texts. Make sure the verses are not taken out of the subject, flow, and context of the passage they were in.

All in All

Perhaps even now, you can start looking into the Bible with "different glasses." You may begin to see things you have not seen before. If you adopt a Fresh-Read approach, you will likely get more out of the Word of God. If you read it as if you had never seen it - take a few minutes to look up odd-sounding phrases or words in other Bible texts - and stop trying to assign meaning to things that are not clearly stated - you will find a much more peaceful and profitable way to read your Bible. You will learn more and be sure of what you glean. What you know will be less debatable, because it is based on just what is written on the page, rather than a theorized version of it.

Chapter 3

It is all Greek to Me

In the Japanese language, some words sound similar but have different meanings. For instance "Ushi" is the Japanese word for "cow", and "oishii" is a common word meaning "tasty" or "delicious." If you were a tourist, I am sure you would not want to eat ice cream, then in your excitement say it tasted like a cow. Thus, pronunciation, definition, and usage are all important when we speak, write, and read.

What about the Bible? Would you say that every translation is completely accurate to the way the original writer intended? Not likely. Depending on the translator or translators, there are going to be times, when a judgment call was made. A phrase or word can have more than one possible meaning, so as a publisher what do you print? Hmm. Of course, each translator is going to write down what they tend to believe, but, translators are human, and every one of them tends to lean certain ways (doctrinally and linguistically).

Ancient

One of the first things we need to understand about the Bible is that it was written a long time ago; especially the first part of the Old Testament. Genesis is dated back to around 1400 BC, and many historians date the book of Job to around 2000 BC or older. The Old Testament books are written in Hebrew-Aramaic, whereas the New Testament books were written in Koine Greek. To get a picture of translation challenges, we need to use our imaginations. Most of us are not translators and pretty much none of us study ancient languages, so we need to go outside our familiar world and delve into some creative thinking.

Imagine that you were digging in your backyard and found a clay pot. The mouth of it is closed up, but when you shake it, you can hear what sounds like something rattling inside it. You work to get the plug out and when you finally get it free, you find some papers inside. When you unroll them, you see they are written in another language. So, you take some pictures and go search the internet to try to identify the language. With some difficulty, you determine that the language is likely a type of Celtic dialect. So, you dutifully search out sources of Celtic dictionaries and buy one. When it is delivered to your door, you are quite excited. You have been waiting for days to unravel the mystery of this old Celtic letter, and you just cannot wait to begin the translation. You grab your trusty translation dictionary of Celtic and begin to write down the English word equivalents. Some symbols are not in the dictionary, so you skip over those. After translating a few phrases, you look at what you have written and it does not make much sense. The words are pretty clear, but the meaning is scrambled and even when you unscramble the order of the words and are pretty sure of the literal translation, it still does not make much sense. Mystified, you go back to the internet and do some more research. You get into forums and investigate blogs until finally, you discover this document is so old that the word meanings have changed. Not only that, but cultural influences have also affected the language, changing subtle nuances. For instance, the meaning of phrases that are more slang-oriented has completely been lost. Similar to our phrase, "It is raining cats and dogs" (which means it is raining very hard), there are slang terms and local word usage that, over time, lost their meaning. Imagine 2000 years from now, someone translating an English document, and trying to figure out why cats and dogs are falling out of the sky. The words are there, but it does not make sense.

When we apply this to our Bibles, we get a different picture of the translation challenges. Biblical Hebrew-Aramaic is difficult enough as it is. It is so old that a single word can have up to fifty or more meanings, thus only the context can be used to determine its probable meaning. In poetic books of the Bible and symbolic prophecies, there are still phrases that the best scholars do not know. The words are there, but the original meaning has been lost. We can read the words, and pray that God helps us understand what the writer was meaning, but as far as the raw translation into an accurate English version, it is just not possible. In some translations of the Bible, the phrases that have lost their original meaning are footnoted.

Now, Greek writing and language are not quite as old, so translations are a little easier. It is also a more exacting language, so accuracy is better. Still, we need to always remember that it is written in ancient Greek, not contemporary Greek. There are also a few slang and culturally influenced phrases that may be hard to accurately translate.

Inerrancy

Bible scholars and ministers have tossed this term (inerrancy) around for centuries, and each of them seems to offer their own definition, but the word simply means without error. Some scholars want to say that the English Translation (mostly King James Version) is without error. Now, I probably will get some blow-back on this, but in plain street language, that is hogwash. Where people are involved there will be errors. Even Jesus' disciples made mistakes. If we did not make mistakes, then we would not need Christ and his salvation. So, let me say this straight. No translation of the Bible is without error.

This brings us to the original manuscript. The first question is this: Do we have access to that? No. We do have very good copies and pieces of documents that date to ancient times. In fact, there are over 5000 documents and pieces that we can look at. When comparing those, there is only a 1% difference. This is good because it appears that there were good and honest people who tried hard to preserve the integrity of the Bible text. So, instead of talking about errors, we should be talking first about the accuracy of the copying – and we can confidently say that was excellent, though not without minor flaws. And the beautiful thing is that none of these minor flaws affect the basic and essential doctrines of God's Word. So, what about the original writing, if we had it in hand? Was it without error?

This depends on your point of view and your definition as well. Here is my take on this and you are free to believe whatever you want: Knowing the character of the people who wrote the Bible and the fact that God selected many of them to be his prophets (spokespersons), I am pretty sure that they did the very best they could to write things down accurately. Whether it was a historical event, lineage, songs, or prophecies, I think God helped them and inspired them. I think he has shown over millenniums that he is pleased with what was written. Is every "the" and "it" dictated by God? No, God gave some men leeway to tell things in their own style, yet correctly. Other men, were instructed exactly what to write. This is true of both the Old and New Testaments.

God's Word

Now here is a sticky wicket. Is the Bible, "God's Word?" Well, I call it that and so do many others. Does this mean if God were to dictate it all it would be the same as it is now? Not likely. God has chosen to use men. So, in a loosely defined manner, we can say that the Bible is absolutely what God wanted us to know, thus, it is his message to us.

> **The message is his, but the actual words used**
> **to relay that message are not all dictated.**

In a real and tangible way, we can rightfully say that even the original manuscript was a translation. God moved on men to write his message, and men took that message and wrote it in their own words, and their language. That is a translation, not a dictation.

The bottom line for us is this: As Christians, we have the Holy Spirit to guide us. Jesus said the Holy Spirit leads us into all truth. So, we have what most in the Old Testament did not have. When we read what God relayed to men, we can sense what God was trying to say to them. We can see the connection to our savior and how it all connects to our lives today – and that is what is the most important to us.

Books, Books, Books

When it comes to studying the Bible, eventually we will want to pull out some reference books to help bring clarity. Several books are good. Some basic study tools can be these:

- Word expository (e.g., W.E. VINE)

- Interlinear (Greek & maybe a Hebrew)

- Exhaustive concordance (Strong's, Thayer, or similar)

Some other books may help from time to time, but these are likely what you will use most of the time. So, let me briefly show you how each can be used.

<u>Word Expository</u>

A word expository is simply an expanded dictionary. You look up a word from the Bible and the expository tells about the word's meaning as it pertains to the original language. It also gives examples of how it is used in several Bible texts. The expose is generally brief, but deep enough for you to get a pretty good idea of what the word meaning is and what it is not.

Interlinear

An interlinear is a handy tool but it helps if you have taken a course in the language (classroom, online, or self-taught). I took a self-taught course in Greek that was called something like "30 minutes a day." It really helped me. I could actually read Greek. I didn't know a lot of words, but I started to understand Biblical texts better.

What is an interlinear? Well, it just puts the Bible text you know, next to the text in the original text language. This works pretty well in Greek, but Hebrew is a lot more challenging. Hebrew reads from right to left, instead of left to right, so following the text is hard. For this reason, I recommend you get the Greek-translated version of the Old Testament. It is called the "Septuagint." It was done by a group of Hebrew scholars (Jews) before Jesus was born. It is pretty accurate and is much easier to cross into English. As far as the New Testament, you will do pretty well using the original Greek for comparing to English.

The big thing to remember when comparing the original text with English is that like most foreign languages, the nouns, verbs, and adjectives, are not in the same order. This is important because most readers will not know the Greek language. The publishers of the interlinear know this, so they put a literal translation of each Greek word below the Greek. So, you will see all the Greek text written out, but right below each word will be the English equivalent of just that word. This means the English below is all choppy and weird sounding. The English words chosen may not even be the best, but it gives you a little glimpse into the exact thought progression of the Bible writer. Seeing the actual ideas as they flow, sometimes helps us understand the intention of the writer, beyond what English translations give us. It helps a little, but you may be able to get similar help by just reading several different translations. Personally, I like the interlinear and I use it frequently. I like to bypass other opinions and see what the original text sounds like. When I can see that the ideas flow better in the original text, then I get the idea that many translations are not doing the writer justice.

<u>Exhaustive Concordance</u>

A Bible Concordance has always been the go-to, for Bible study. It is just a simple reverse index to tell you where a word occurs in the Bible. The Strong's is both a concordance and a brief dictionary or "lexicon." This is a very handy tool because if you want to see verses that have a specific word in them, you can see a large list of references. If you are looking for a specific topic, it can help you prepare a teaching on the subject. Of course, there are better tools for preparing lessons. A topical Bible is much easier to use than a concordance for searching topics.

Better Ways

Okay, let's bring this up to the twenty-first century. Honestly, I think the very best way to use reference books is to look up the information on the internet. A well-worded search brings up some very good information and many online Bible tools that are free. So, yes, you can go out and buy the clunky books that weigh a ton, or you can get digital apps, but I use a search engine more than anything else. And as far as a Concordance goes, if I just put the word "Bible" in the search engine and then a word or phrase, I always get results within a second. I can use "interlinear" and then a scripture reference, and bam, I get links where I can view that. Now, if I want to know everywhere in the Bible a certain word or phrase occurs, I find the internet searches are sadly not up to the task. I do not get complete results. So, I obtained a pdf version of the Bible (actually free), and I can do any word or phrase search - and I can see every place those occur. So the drudgery of looking through big books or booting up a computer is so yesterday. Just dig into the digital world, and use technology to get the answers immediately. Oh, and it really cuts down on sermon-making time, too. ☺

When Books Fail

Regardless of the source you use to explore the original text language, there is a danger. Even if I use the very best word expository, there can be pitfalls. And, if I just use an interlinear or concordance dictionary, I can get into real trouble. Why? Because we are talking about translating ideas, not words. How many times in your life have you been misunderstood? Did you use the wrong words, or were your words not understood the way you intended? So, when it comes to the Bible, we need to know what the writer was saying. We can take a microscope and study each word very closely, and still miss what the writer was trying to say. So, be very careful to see word definitions as a means to understanding the whole passage, not a pivot point that forces meaning into the entire text. Word meanings are pieces to a puzzle, not the entire mosaic.

The very best Bible studies are about determining the central idea of a whole scripture passage. Specific isolated verses can be misleading. This is why verses should never be used out of context. They should never stand alone. Context is very important in all languages, and in some cases, it is critical.

Perhaps a little side-light here: At the writing of this book, I am having apologetic style debates with scholars, nearly every day, and I find it interesting when my peers nail down word definitions in the Old Testament and then build a doctrine around that idea. I seem to constantly be reminding others that the Old Testament was written over 1400 years before Christ. Even in Jesus' time, the language was ancient and word meanings had changed. Trying to firmly nail down definitions in an extremely old language, where even the best experts do not agree on word meanings is just not possible.

A Word about Commentaries

I suppose before I finish this section, I will end up on my soap box, preaching, complaining, or something. You see, the idea of using commentaries is a sore subject for me. I have seen ministers, lay teachers, scholars, Bible study leaders, and more quote commentaries consistently. The commentaries that are mostly used are the ones printed within the covers of the Bible itself. This is handy, but it tends to give credibility to someone's writing. I do not believe that a man's opinion is anywhere close to equal to scripture.

I see the value of good scholars sharing what they have learned and how they see Bible text, but I think we need to put the commentaries in perspective. They have a rightful place, but they should stay in that place, in our minds and hearts. My take on all this is like this:

Even expert commentaries are still the opinion of one man.

So, yes, do use commentaries as a reference. But, first, read the Bible without it and know the text thoroughly, without it. On the written content alone, and considering the underlying language, and who it was written to, judge the probable meaning. Once you believe you have a firm grasp on what the writer said and what he did not say, then look at a commentary to see how someone else views the text. But, you be the final judge of what the text says. You determine whether the commentator's ideas line up with the actual written text or not. Never let "experts" bully you into one way of thinking. Always go back to the text and to other verses that teach the same thing, and let the Bible define itself. Do all you can to make the Bible speak for itself. If a commentary seems to stretch the meaning, impose meaning or twist the simplicity of the content, then throw that comment out.

Chapter 4

Very Old History

One fine summer day, Grandma and Grandpa were sitting and discussing the good-ole-days. They would mention some things their kids did and then laugh. As time went on, Grandpa recalled a vacation the family had enjoyed. He said, "And, I remember when Bobby slid down that muddy trail into the lake and ripped the leg off of his pants." Grandma said, "That was not the way it happened. It was our daughter, Melinda, and she was on that rope swing over the lake." Then Grandma and Grandpa went from laughing to arguing and the debate became quite heated. Eventually, Grandma made a kind of huffing sound, got up, went into the kitchen, and asked if anyone was hungry.

On a larger scale, when the entire history of the world is considered, no two historians agree how everything happened. So, who is right? Hmm. Maybe nobody. There is no way we can go back in time and personally view everything that has happened. Thus, we must rely on circumstantial evidence and written accounts of the people who were there. Are these accurate? No. Experts tend to agree that even eyewitness testimony can be unreliable. In the other arena, circumstantial evidence can also be misleading. There is no way to know what pieces of a puzzle are missing when artifacts are found, and we may not even know in what order things happen, even when clues are left behind. Perhaps a rather feeble example might be something like this:

Riddle:

A crime was committed, and when it was investigated, the facts seem to surround these clues: Inside a locked room, there was a dead body, laying on the floor. Near the body were broken glass and some water. In the corner of the room, there was a black cat. Other than furniture, there was no other significant crime information. It was noted, however, that there did not seem to be any signs of forced entry.

Solve the crime.

Now many people have scratched their heads over this riddle, while others know immediately what happened. The key to solving it is to not make assumptions. So, what happened? Have you unlocked the mystery yet?

The first false assumption that most people make is that the dead body is human. If we get past that idea, the rest of the story comes easily. Here is what happened. The cat knocked over the fishbowl and the dead body on the floor is a fish.

Now, what if, this tale was real and it was passed around to people, without the knowledge of what happened? I think you can imagine what rumors of murder would be spread around town. It might even make it into local news reports.

Bible

When it comes to the Bible, history is important. In fact, it is critical. If we ignore history, we will misinterpret the Bible and receive it in a light that God never intended. A lot of the Old Testament includes accounts of things that happened. There is the creation of the world and all the creatures here. There is the creation of mankind, his falling away from God, and how God dealt with people's treachery. It logs the development of a whole nation from the lineage of Abraham and how God made a contract with them, like with no other nation. There is the rise and fall of many kings, and whether they followed God or not. There are parts of the Old Testament that have many of the things God's prophets said to Israel about their future.

What is missing in the Old Testament are things that are specifically directed to America in the twenty-first century. They are just not there. The same is true for the New Testament. There is no specific direction to America or the church in our century. The books in the Bible were originally written for people of their day to read, and for them to live by. So, why do we read it? I think it is pretty easy to see that our best use of the Bible is to see how God interfaced with mankind, over thousands of years, so we can know who God is and what he expects from people. When we see him reward nations and people for doing what is right, we can know that he will treat us the same. One thing we can learn about God in the Bible is that he says he never changes. He is the same today as he was then. This means that though to some people the Bible does not seem relevant, God is definitely relevant. And if he is relevant, to you and me today, then all of what he has ever done, has relevance in our lives. So, we can look into the Bible and see nearly countless examples of what we should and should not do. We can see that God cares about how people act toward him and each other. Even in the New Testament, the directions to Jesus' followers were for them, yet because Jesus is alive and the same person today, we can learn from what they were told. Many, if not all, of the directives given to the disciples and the early church, apply to our lives. Spirituality, morality, love for each other, and so much more, are the same messages for us today, even millennia later. Is everything that happened with people in the Bible applicable to each of us today? No. Because one man was told to go wash in a pool to be healed, does not mean we tell everyone to go wash in that same pool. Jesus did not direct that to us. In fact, there is no Biblical record I can find that Jesus told more than one person to go wash in the pool. God does work with us individually, as well as corporately. Today, we read and pray and we glean the good things of God from his Word. We apply everything possible to our lives, trying hard not to miss anything that applies.

Another important ingredient in this whole subject is the idea of pulling out texts and using them as personal promises. Though it can give us warm fuzzies, it is not a good way to apply God's Word to our life. One glaring example that I frequently bring up, is the promises that God gave Israel (if they followed him). If you look in the book of Exodus, you will find that when the Israelites were at Mt Sinai, God made huge promises to them and only them – no other nation. As time went on, Israel broke the contract, over and over. Again and again, God would allow them to resume the contract if they would come back and follow him. This renewal throughout the Old Testament confuses Bible readers today. Here is a classic example:

> **2 Chronicles 7:14 - If my people, who are called by my name, will humble themselves and pray and seek my face and turn from their wicked ways, then I will hear from heaven, and I will forgive their sin and will heal their land.**

This has been used so many times in our century to rally the church to prayer. It has been used in politically motived meetings also to forward certain notions. However, this is God telling the children of Jacob (Israel) that he would honor his original promise to them if they would come back and serve him. At that point, Israel had become corrupt and they worshipped everything but God. Some of their idol worship included sacrificing children in the fire. It was horrible. God told them if they would stop what they were doing, humble themselves before him (obey him), and pray (ask him to forgive them and pledge themselves to him), that he would heal their land and restore their nation. What is important here is to see that this promise was only made to them. God never made this promise to any other nation, at any other time, for all of the

Bible's recorded history, through about 100 AD. Thus, it is inappropriate for us in America, 3400 years later to claim that God has promised this to us. He has not. Does this mean God has not and will not bless America? No. America is blessed because Christians have been salt and light to our nation. We have influenced the nation with our Godliness and if that ever stops or diminishes, we will see the bad effect. When American as a whole recognizes God and his importance to the country, God blesses them, and yes part of that blessing is protection. In contrast, if we trust in our wisdom and our weapons, and say we do not need God, then God may remove a level of protection that could have been there. But, this has nothing to do with any promise that God made to Israel.

Diving In

To see how the historical portions of the Old Testament apply to us and how they do not, I want to show you some examples. First, let's look at Joshua, chapter 6.

> **Now the gates of Jericho were securely**
> **barred because of the Israelites. No one went**
> **out and no one came in. 2 Then the Lord**
> **said to Joshua, "See, I have delivered Jericho**
> **into your hands, along with its king and its**
> **fighting men. 3 March around the city once**
> **with all the armed men. Do this for six days.**
> **4 Have seven priests carry trumpets of rams'**
> **horns in front of the ark. On the seventh**
> **day, march around the city seven times, with**
> **the priests blowing the trumpets. 5 When**
> **you hear them sound a long blast on the**

**trumpets, have the whole army give a loud
shout; then the wall of the city will collapse
and the army will go up, everyone straight
in."**

It is a pretty interesting story, right? But, the really big
question of all this is, does this scripture apply to me in the 21st
century? Hmm. Maybe it does, but the more important
question is this: Is the word of the Lord, directed to me,
personally? It was God himself that directed Joshua to do this,
but is the validity of God's word, reason enough to apply his
direction to me, in all cases? In other words, because God told
Joshua to "march around the city," does this mean that God
wants us to march around that city or any other? The answer
is, no. You see, my dear friend, not every directive God has
ever given to a person or a nation, was or is meant for us to
obey. There are certain commands and directives in the Bible
that are clearly for the church of Jesus Christ. The church is
still in existence, so those directives do apply to us as part of
that body. However, the other directives in the Bible must be
viewed as second-hand lessons. We can see how God worked
with other people and we can see how they responded. From
the lessons so many other people learned, we can glean
information about who God is, how he operates, and what he
expects from us as a human race.

This discussed scenario has been a big problem within the
church world. Some scholars want to say that nothing in the
Bible is directly for us and it is all to be spiritualized. Other
scholars insist that everything within the pages of the Bible
should be taken literally. This includes ideas that every
command in the Bible is directed to us and is for us. Now, it

does not take a huge amount of study to begin seeing the flaws in both of these highly polarized positions. If everything is only a spiritual lesson, then Jesus did not come to this world physically and die on a physical cross. In contrast, if every command is directed to us, then we better get busy marching around cities. But, there is another path, and that is to just read God's Word, like a book, and take it for what it says. Read others' experiences and learn from their mistakes. Believe what Jesus said and follow it – just as the early followers did. See dreams and visions others have had as just that. They are symbolic views (not view screens) about their future - not necessarily ours.

Today, there is yet another group of believers that have decided on a kind of half-way version of personal direction. This group thinks that if they pick up certain practices of Bible passages it will gain them favor with God, or move some kind of spiritual mountain. For example, Christian leaders may gather a large group of believers and march around an object, neighborhood, or even a whole city, to overcome the evil forces of the devil, or to claim the territory for God and his kingdom. While I can appreciate the energy and the symbolic effort, at the end of the day it is just silliness when it comes to accomplishing what they claim. There is absolutely nothing in God's Word that directs the church to practice such things. The ideas are imported from Joshua's success at Jericho, over 3500 years ago. It has no bearing on spiritual warfare today, and there is no such thing as claiming the land for the church or the kingdom of God. Neither Christ nor his disciples practiced such nonsense. And, let me point out that since the conquest of Jericho, there is nothing recorded in scripture about God ever using this tactic again. In plain talk: God only directed someone to march around a city, once – never again. So, let me say this rather empathically:

There is nothing magical, nor Godly about marching around things.

This whole idea is once more an attempt to put power and control in people's hands. It is people trying to manipulate God, or some other kind of power, to do their will. The Bible says this is tempting God. Here is the bold-faced truth:

If God has not specifically directed us to act, then we cannot claim that he is or will be backing what we do.

Mini-Summary

To ensure you are understanding the point of what we just discussed, let me help you digest all of this. When we are doing a Fresh Read of the Bible, we are looking for what the book says, not what we want it to say. We also do not want to see the Bible as a book of spells or incantations. Okay, yes, some readers may say, "Pastor! How could you even suggest such a thing?" My answer to that is this: I have seen this kind of "witchery" done with God's Word for a very long time. So, before we all get our brains in a tizzy, let's look at this situation from a very practical point of view. Example: If I open God's Word and pick out a verse, take that and say, "I will practice this, because it is God's Word, "then use that principle as a guarantee of success, it turns God's Word into a book of spells. We are saying to ourselves that if we speak the written words in the Bible, we will have the same power as God. We are saying it is words that make things happen, and God has never said that. For example, if there is a text where God tells a prophet that it will rain tomorrow, I cannot and should not take that verse and quote it, thinking that it has the power to make it rain tomorrow. This is called usurping power from God and God will not stand for any human being wielding his power autonomously. God will not back that sinful behavior. Again, the Bible says this is tempting God and it is sin! And let me be clear here. Trying to make it rain is a drop in the bucket (no pun intended) when it comes to how people use scripture for their own gain. There are whole groups of people who constantly take scripture and use it in a way that is similar to white witchcraft. As witches do, they try to influence spiritual forces to do their will. And yes, "white witches" have and do use the name and character of Christ in their spells and for getting "guidance." Will Jesus help them? No. But they think he is. Am I saying this because of what I imagine, or maybe from a book someone wrote? Is this just Christian propaganda? No. I have a Christian friend who was once in white witchcraft and she was the one who told me about their practices and about what she used to do. She said at one point she was encouraged to choose a spiritual force to guide her and give her power. Of all those she could have chosen, she chose Jesus. Not to have a personal savior relationship, but to look to him as her mystical and spiritual guide. She even had a real vision of a figure that looked exactly like Jesus (as she imagined him). After she gave her life to Christ, she realized that the figure she saw was not the real Jesus. The bottom line to all this is a directive I would like to give you all. The Bible is a book to be read, in context, in order of normal flow. It is not a book of separate verses to be used for gain or to manipulate heaven into doing your will. And when I say "your will," I mean even when your will is attached to the name of Jesus or his Father, God. Just because you tack on the name of God, does not mean you are doing his will. History is replete with examples of Christians doing terrible things in the "name of Jesus." And, it is my opinion that many of those who called themselves Christians and performed those acts had no true relationship with Christ. I do not believe that a truly born-again believer could consistently do terrible things to other human beings. It is not in the character of Christ or his Spirit that dwells within us.

An Overview of other Examples

There are nearly countless examples of Old Testament scriptures that people have misused and misunderstood, and there is no way I can present all those in this book. Instead, I want to just mention a few obvious stories and situations.

<u>War</u>

There are many instances where God told the nation of Israel to war against another nation. He told them to conquer them, and in some cases, wipe them out. Now there were several reasons why God has Israel do this to those specific nations. What God did not tell them to do is conquer the world or be brutal to all people. God was selective in how he chose the destruction of some very evil nations, and he chose Israel to be their judge.

When we read these things, we might even cringe. It is hard for people in a civilized age (especially prosperous nations) to understand why this kind of destruction was necessary, but it was. We can compare this to the way many people today believe that Hitler needed to be overthrown and killed. He was evil at heart and authored the death of millions of innocent people. If we can take this idea and export it to the early days of Israel, we can see that evil nations were hurting a lot of innocent people and practicing some very vile things – and growing even worse in their practices and beliefs.

I think when we read these things, most Christians would not pick up these commands as a call to war. Now, if our country was attacked, there might be some ministers who would pull out one of these texts and claim that God says to go to war, but that would be a very wrong use of scripture. God has given each country the right to defend its borders. We do not need to misuse scripture so when we fight, we think it is the "Christian" or "Godly" thing to do. It may or may not be, but our beliefs should not be based on texts that were directed at a different country, with a different circumstance in very ancient history. Even common sense tends to lean away from such thinking.

<u>Abraham and Isaac</u>

Oh, people love to get ahold of this passage of scripture and ministers have found plenty of sermon fodder here. In case you are unfamiliar with this story in Genesis 22, God tells Abraham to take his promised son to the mountain and sacrifice him there. Pretty horrible, right? But, God wanted to see if Abraham had the same heart as He did. God was going to give up his only son to death, and Abraham was going to be the father of the nation that birthed God's son. Abraham was also considered to be the "friend of God," so there was a deep connection between God and Abraham. At no other time did

God command this kind of sacrifice, so we know there was something very special going on.

Now, some Christians will want to take this and try to import it into our lives today. Some might even say we need to sacrifice our children for the better good. Along this line of reasoning, even abortion could be justified, but this is not the work of God. The Holy Spirit does not require women to abort their babies for the greater good, and Isaac should never be used as a correlation to abortion.

In other applications of this scripture, things can get pretty twisted - so again, we need to be very careful not to take God's command to an Old Testament person, and apply it directly to our Christian lives today. This is just plain bad Bible Study.

<u>Moses Parts the Waters</u>

Last, but not least, is the parting of the Red Sea (Exodus 14). First, let me say that it was not likely the Red Sea that Moses and the Children of Israel crossed. It was much more likely the Sea of Reeds, which (if you look at a map) was a major body of water that stood in the way when trekking to Mt Sinai.

As a reminder, Moses and the offspring of Israel (Jacob), were leaving Egypt. After leaving, the Pharaoh changed his mind about letting them go and started chasing them with his army. Moses and the people came to the Sea of Reeds and could go no farther. The enemy was behind them and the sea was in front of them. God told Moses to stretch out his staff and when he did the waters parted so everyone could walk across on dry ground. Then God closed up the waters behind them, drowning Pharaoh's army.

Can this situation and this miracle be directly applied to the church today? Hmm. Well, good Christians do try. Many try to spiritualize this miracle and then apply it to a current situation. They feel that if they remind God of what he did, and then tell God to do the same for them in a situation, God is bound to do it. You have probably heard these kinds of prayers: "Lord, we know you parted the waters at the Red Sea, so push back the waters of this flood." So, is this a good prayer? Well, maybe there is nothing wrong with the actual words. It is more about the focus. If I am quoting scripture to get God to do things for me, there could be a problem with my heart. Instead, if I am saying to God, "I know what you did back then, and because of that, I can believe in you and your care for me," then I am trusting in God, personally. This is an indication that my heart and my relationship with God are right. As Christians, we should never try to push God into doing things for us. This is selfish and violates the basis of our close and tender relationship with him. All we need to do is ask him and trust in his character and in the relationship we have with him.

The best Bible reading is born from a desire to know who God is, and to draw close to him.

Chapter 5

Lay Down the Law

When I went to Bible College, I had a class called "Old Testament Survey." It was about as interesting as watching moss grow. I did have the desire to know what was in God's Word and I wanted to be able to teach it rightly, but this was a two-hour class and it was super boring. The instructor was dull as dull can be. I remember dozing off many times in that class and feeling embarrassed about it. Of course, we had no energy drinks yet, and I was not a fan of coffee, so caffeine was not in my diet plan. If I was doing that class today, I would be engaging in some alertness techniques. However, to give you an idea about this course, it was not about the actual scriptural content of the Bible, it was an overview of what each book was about and, I think, the era in which they were written. I remember that one of our tests (the final) included listing all the books of the Old Testament in their proper order and spelling them correctly. Let me tell you that is quite a challenge, especially if you are working after school and having trouble just getting time for homework - but I aced it. Was there a benefit? Well, even many years later, I can still pretty much recite the order of those books. Most or all I can spell as well. So, as boring as it was, there seemed to be some value in it. In case you may be interested, I have some books in my church office library that are surveys of the Bible and its books. So, come on by.

Okay, in all honesty, that was supposed to be an interesting story, but I am not at all sure that it was any better than the class I took on the Old Testament - so, if you tended to fall asleep during my little story, feel free to go get some coffee, or snack, or whatever. I will wait.

The Law

The Mosaic Law, often just called "the Law," is first found in the book of Exodus and it is covered in about nine chapters (21-24 & 31-35). This is the basics of the Law, but over time, the priests and leaders of Israel added more details. In Jesus' time, there were about 600 laws. Besides the basic laws for everyone, there were also details about how the priests were to perform their duties. For these, we look into the book of Leviticus.

Since the Law covers so much territory, what is the best way to study it? Right now, there are probably some readers who are feeling anxious. There are so many rules with dos and don'ts that the Law just gets tiresome and in some cases, really over the top. So, how do we quell all this internal jitter? Well, it starts here: If we use our Fresh Read technique and implement our RID rules, we can glean some good and easy things. When we go through the Law, what we are not going to do is to assign meaning or importance to it. We are going to read it with curiosity. We want to know what God told Moses and Israel, about 3400 years ago. What we are not going to do, is see every verse as something that God is speaking to us personally, today. When we see a verse that says not to eat pork and to only observe Saturday as the worship day, we are not going to feel guilty and decide that the Bible is telling us to do this. The same Bible we are reading, tells us that Christ fulfilled all of the Law when he went to the cross and died for us. If we accept Christ's sacrifice and believe he died for us (personally) then this old Law no longer touches us. It is no longer in effect and has no power over us. In fact, to try to observe the Law and keep it would be a slap in Jesus' face. In a real sense, it would make a statement that what Jesus did was not enough and that we need to "help" with our salvation. We do not, and should not.

Value

What value is there in reading the Law, then? To answer this, let me tell you what I get out of it. And, no, this does not mean it will be what you glean from it. As I always say, you have to make up your mind, based on the evidence.

When I see God telling what the Israelites need to do, I see a set of parameters that were designed to keep them safe: Safe from disease; safe from internal strife; and safe from their enemies. As a good parent, God is setting down good rules, so they would be preserved as a nation and as a race. The stark truth is that many other nations and communities had been wiped out by plagues and diseases. Bacteria, viruses, and war destroyed them. No one had a clue what caused disease and God felt it was better to give the cure of prevention, rather than try to educate an ancient culture about tiny bugs that no one could see. The result of the Law was that the nation was preserved for a long time. It eventually split and basically, only the tribe of Judah and some Levites survived. The whole plan of God was to preserve the nation because the Messiah would come from it. Even though the Israelites rebelled against God many times, God still preserved the race until Jesus could be born. Sadly, after about 70AD, not many Jews were left, and the nation was finally decimated. In contrast, the Messiah lived and still does. This is called success. God never fails.

Time to Focus

To put this Fresh Read into practice, we need to zero in on a few texts and see some methods of study. If you will put on your patience hat for a few minutes, I will dive into some passages in the Law that could cause us some concern.

Here are the first two lines of the law (after the Ten Commandments):

> **Exodus 21:2-3 --- "If you buy a Hebrew servant, he is to serve you for six years. But in the seventh year, he shall go free, without paying anything. If he comes alone, he is to go free alone; but if he has a wife when he comes, she is to go with him."**

Now, what is the first thing to do when we see this passage? For our study purposes, we need to adopt some simple guidelines, so we are going to see how our RID rules work for this scripture. First, we read it straight and fresh. We do not assume anything when we read it. We do not assign a meaning that we heard or learned. We read it as if we have never seen it. I encourage you to do this, right now. When you read it a few seconds ago, if you already assigned it meaning, then go back and read it again, and see the text for only what it says (no other background). Here is what I get from this scripture: It appears to be talking to someone who can buy a slave that is the same race as the people who are being addressed. In our time and in America, it would be like saying, "If you buy a slave that is American." The scripture has an even deeper meaning, however, because it talks about race, not just nationality. Since Americans can be any race, it would be more like saying to a full-blooded German American, "If you buy a German-American slave." Now, in America, it is very distasteful to even talk about having a slave, so this whole idea is repulsive to most of us. In fact, we can get bogged down when reading this part of the Law and not want to go on reading. But let's consider the context of this passage. The Hebrews (Children of Israel), just came from Egypt. For a long time, they had all been slaves to the Egyptians. So slavery was not a foreign idea to them. Slavery may have been much more accepted as a normal function of society.

What is quite different from Egyptian slavery are the terms of enslavement. God told them that they could not keep a fellow countryman enslaved for more than 6 years and that if his wife was enslaved with him, she was to go free also. What seems to be clear to me is that slavery was allowed, but with exacting limitations – however, you may read this differently. Your opinion is as valid as anyone's, as long as you do not insert ideas into the text that are not there.

The second rule of RID is to see if there is anything that sounds weird; that is, odd phrasing or images. If there are, then we need to look elsewhere in the Bible, where the same terms occur. So, when you read this passage in Exodus, do you see anything that is not readily understood? Are there words or phrases that do not make sense? I would say, no, but if you see anything, then do a digital search of the entire Bible text and see if the word or phrase occurs in another passage of scripture. See how it is used there and you might get a clue to the meaning of the words in this Mosaic Law passage.

The third rule of RID comes into play when we cannot readily see the meaning of a word or phrase. The rule is, don't play God. Some things in scripture are symbols that God did not explain. If God did not tell us, then we need to leave it as a mystery – at least until we can find other scripture that gives us clues. I would say that this passage in Exodus is pretty clear, so we do not have to worry about playing God here.

Finally, we need to ask if this passage is directed at the church, and especially the church in the twenty-first century. What do you think? Well, here is my response to that question: First, I do not believe that it is possible to buy a full-blooded Hebrew person or even a half-blooded Hebrew person. The Hebrew children were so scattered through other countries for thousands of years and they have intermarried other races so many times, that there are no true Hebrews. In fact, no one has yet been able to trace DNA back to most, if not all, of the children of Israel. We see people who are practicing Judaism and are called Jews, but many of them can be traced back to Turkey, not directly to Israel or Hebrew descent. If I am wrong, that is fine, I have been wrong before, but what I said is what I found when trying to trace Hebrew lineage. Even if you or I could buy a Hebrew slave, would we? No, of course not. This idea is completely foreign to the Christian church in America. In addition, we are no longer under the Law. Christ fulfilled the Law, so it does not touch us. We are led by the Holy Spirit and under the grace of the New Covenant. So this law, given by God, is not directed at us, at all. When we read this it should be received as what "used to be."

There is one last thing I want to leave with you about this passage. Whenever we read the Law, we should see God's heart and the parameters of his perfection. We see how holy he is, and see his intolerance for sin. In a real sense, we get to see his measuring stick for human beings. Though we are not under the Law, we should never forget how much God hates sin and how he abhors certain behaviors. When we look into the Law, we should side with God, and try very hard to keep with the same moral code as God has described. We no longer have the punishment of the Law, nor should we ever consider criticizing someone or bringing our judgment on them. This is wrong and a sin in itself. At the same time, we should never say or consider that what God has said is wrong, is right. If in God's Law, he said that a man should not have sex with another man, then we must not say it is right, even though we do not bring the Law and its punishment down on a man who does have sex with another. The Law can now be seen as a guide to see God's desire for mankind to live free from sin. We can look into the Law and hear God's heart, then take that into our own lives. We use it to draw near to God and to want to please him. We internalize the Law, not to keep it, but to understand the intricacies of our maker and our savior.

Sample #2

I think we mashed on the first two lines of the Law long enough, so let's look at another part of the Law.

Exodus 21:12-17 & 22-24 --- 12 "Anyone who strikes a person with a fatal blow is to be put to death. 13 However, if it is not done intentionally, but God lets it happen, they are to flee to a place I will designate. 14 But if anyone schemes and kills someone deliberately, that person is to be taken from my altar and put to death. 15 "Anyone who attacks their father or mother is to be put to death. 16 "Anyone who kidnaps someone is to be put to death, whether the victim has been sold or is still in the kidnapper's possession. 17 "Anyone who curses their father or mother is to be put to death.

22 "If people are fighting and hit a pregnant woman and she gives birth prematurely but there is no serious injury, the offender must be fined whatever the woman's husband demands and the court allows. 23 But if there is serious injury, you are to take life for life, 24 eye for eye, tooth for tooth, hand for

**hand, foot for foot, 25 burn for burn, wound
for wound, bruise for bruise.**

Okay, now we do a Fresh Read of this and see if it makes
sense. Most of this seems to be pretty plain in the NIV version,
and I think it will be plain in most other translations also. The
older King James versions could be pretty choppy.

First, I see that if a person hits someone else, and he ends up
dying, the hitter is to be executed - but only if he meant to kill
the other person. What seems unfamiliar in western culture is
that it sounds like there is a place for this person (the hitter) to
go for safety. This raises two questions:

1. Why would an innocent person need protection?

2. Where is this safe place, and what kind of place is it?

In our RID rules, this situation qualifies as the "I" in the
acronym: "If it sounds weird, look it up." So this is what you
will need to do. Using digital searches in Bible software,
searching online, or doing a "find" in a pdf version of the Bible
are all good ways to explore. Also, a simple search for terms
like "sanctuary" and "refuge" can help. To be honest, these
questions are fairly easily answered, but simple searches may
not produce many answers. If, however, you search for
something like this: "Bible: City of Refuge" you will get more
results. Here is what I found:

**Numbers 35: - 9 Then the Lord said to
Moses: 10 "Speak to the Israelites and say to
them: 'When you cross the Jordan into
Canaan, 11 select some towns to be your**

**cities of refuge, to which a person who has
killed someone accidentally may flee. 12
They will be places of refuge from the
avenger, so that anyone accused of murder
may not die before they stand trial before the
assembly.**

Here in the Book of Numbers, we see the description of these
safe places and why they were needed. These were six cities
that were set up to protect those who killed someone and were
to stand trial. These places of refuge protected the hitter until
they could stand trial. To me, it sounds like in the public eye,
or at least to the family of the person who was killed, the hitter
was assumed guilty of murder until proven innocent by a court
of law – but you see what you think. I suppose today, we
would call this protective custody. We do not have cities of
refuge, instead, we would probably put them in jail or a Safe
House.

As far as a Fresh Read, this passage was problematic. The
answers were available in the Bible, but they were not in the
area we were reading. Even reading through the book of
Exodus would not have given us the answers. As I said before,
even searching for some of the words or phrases in our text
may not have given us any helpful results. We had a couple of
choices: We could have just made a note about this passage
and kept reading the Bible. Eventually, we would have
stumbled upon the answer. However, if we looked at some
cross-references for this text, we would have found the answer
more quickly. So, let me say that there are Bible reference
tools that give cross reference to nearly every verse in the
Bible. The best of these tools is what is called a "Reference

Bible." The Thompson Chain Bible is an example of one of the most useful and well-respected Bibles available. Next to each verse, as you read, there are one or more references to other texts that talk about a similar topic. So, when we get confused about the terms in a verse, we can go to the other cross-referenced texts and we may get more clarity there. Let me say, however, that these cross-references are still educated guesses of what verses go with other verses. So, word and phrase searches in the Bible are sometimes more valuable, in that you are not restricted to just cross-references that someone else thinks go together. In the case of the refuge cities, I am sure that reference Bibles will help lead you to the other passages that explain what they are.

The next thing I see in this passage is the consequences of physically attacking a child's mother or father. It is death. What is interesting here is that there is no recourse. This does not say that the child killed their father or mother, but it may be implied from the subject matter in the verses before it. However, if we take this as written, it sure sounds like attacking a mother or father, even if it was not to kill them, resulted in execution. One thing we do see in the Old Testament is that under the Law, rebellion against the authority of any kind was usually met with execution. Rebellion was just not tolerated.

I do not see anything odd to look up for this text. It seems pretty clear, with possibly a nagging question of whether the child had to be trying to kill his parents, verses just hitting them. I do not think doing word searches is going to help, and I doubt even cross-references will give us a full answer. So, I say, we leave it as is and take it as it was written, at least until we read something later that may clarify.

Moving on through this text, we come to kidnapping. My first impression is this: Who would even dream that kidnapping would be in the Bible? Hmm. Well, it looks like it is an important law. The text reads pretty clearly to me. If you kidnap anyone, you are to be executed. Now, if you get something else from this, that is okay, but it looks pretty uncluttered to me. A Fresh Read is probably enough for this text. It does not seem to have any weird words or phrasing.

The last thing we want to explore is its value in today's world. Though this Law is no longer in effect for today's church, the principle can be carried forward to guide our current laws. With all the child abduction and sex trafficking, I have to wonder if it would be as bad if there was capital punishment for kidnapping. Hmm.

Okay, what about the next portion of this scripture? It is about cursing your parents and the penalty. Of course, this would be the opposite of the Ten Commandments that instruct us to honor our father and mother. The penalty for violating this commandment is death, at least when it comes to cursing them. Now, to me this verse has clear phrasing, so we do not need to look anything up – except possibly its correlation to the Ten Commandments (Exodus 20). However, since we are on the subject, it might be beneficial to think about this passage:

> **Mark 7: - 10 For Moses said, 'Honor your father and mother,' and, 'Anyone who curses their father or mother is to be put to death.'**
> **11 But you say that if anyone declares that**

**what might have been used to help their
father or mother is Corban (that is, devoted
to God)— 12 then you no longer let them do
anything for their father or mother. 13 Thus
you nullify the word of God by your tradition
that you have handed down. And you do
many things like that."**

In this text, Jesus quotes the verse in Exodus. When we have a direct quoted linked to another verse in the Bible, then we can rightfully connect their ideas to establish proper doctrine. This is proper. However, if we connected two verses that we want to be together to establish some theory of our own, then we can create a new doctrine that could be wrong. My advice is to be very careful connecting verses in the Bible that are not specifically connected by the original writer. Also, be extremely careful to not entertain doctrines that someone else has built, using a technique where several texts are referenced as the same idea, when the writers may not have intended for their writing to be connected in that way. End-times (Eschatology) theories often use this method to create doctrines that are more fanciful than fact.

Finally, in this scripture passage, we come to the place where pregnant women are protected. This passage seems to mostly be based on a situation where people are fighting. What I see from the text is that if a pregnant woman gets hit and it causes an early delivery, then as long as there was no serious injury, the hitter is not executed. The hitter does have to pay a fine according to what the husband requires. I think there may be some leeway here for no serious injury to the child, either, but the text is not clear about that. It sounds to me that it is focused more on the mother's health. So, we do not have all the facts. I think searching for more clarity on this will not produce a better understanding, but as far as the child itself, we would need to search the Bible and cross-references to see what laws cover child protection.

It seems to me this situation with a pregnant woman has to do with a fight that breaks out in the proximity of the woman. Perhaps this could happen in the marketplace or the woman's home. The location is not defined in the Law. What also does not seem to be covered here is domestic disputes. This law does not address a fight between a husband and a wife. We would need to look at the rest of the Law to see if there are any texts covering domestic disputes. Word and phrase searches can be helpful, but those cross-referenced texts may be quicker. Since this book is about how to study and not a commentary, I am not going to do this research for you. You need to go forth and conquer.

Tidy Up

When it comes to Old Testament (Mosaic) Law, we cannot fully understand all the implications. It was written to be understood by people in a completely different culture and at an ancient time in history. The framework for God's laws was well within the requirements of laws that existed in other places at their time. What I mean is that there were also laws in other nations that were brutal. There were often executions for doing wrongs that are less severely punished in our American culture. Leaders of nations and empires ruled by terror. They purposely wanted to strike terror into the hearts of their subjects, so there would be no rebellion. They also did not want ramped violence or civil disobedience. Thus, the consequence of disobeying many laws was a swift and brutal death. When a whole group of people or a nation has been conditioned to respond to this methodology, it would be impossible to keep civil order by giving someone tongue-lashings or a few days of jail time. People would not obey the laws or have respect for the leadership. So, was God such a mean guy, or was he establishing laws that were based on what the people in that time and culture needed? Hmm. You be the judge, but I think if you go and read the history of that period and especially look at how justice was doled out, you will see how brutal most justice systems were.

Lastly, let me caution you against importing twenty-first-century American culture and justice into ancient culture. It just does not work, and it creates improper judgment on what we cannot understand. It is the right attitude to look into the ancient text of the Bible and accept it fully, while still saying, "I do not understand why things were the way they were." This is proper Bible Study. We can continue to seek more understanding of that culture and the period, but frankly, we can never walk in their shoes or experience what they did. We should not try. The best thing we can do is read the text and try to see how they responded to what was happening. Always remember this:

> **You will never understand everything that is written in the Bible. However, the main things are plain.**

Chapter 6

The Value of Songs

I have enjoyed being an electronics technician since I was about 16 years old. It is a great hobby and, at times, it was my livelihood. At one time, I had a stereo repair shop, and people would bring me all kinds of sound equipment to fix. Guess what? I fixed them all (if the customer had the funds). Now, one of the perks of that business is that sometimes people also want to sell their equipment – and sometimes rather cheaply. These opportunities included stereo equipment, but also sound reinforcement equipment (PA heads, etc.).

About now, you might be asking yourself, why would an electronics technician need sound equipment? Well, during this period of my life I was wanting to record myself. There were people in my church that decided they liked my singing voice, and I was even asked if I had recorded anything. So, I pursued trying to improve my vocals and recording them. I also wanted to record some of my music for my mother. Over time, I obtained some recording equipment, microphones, and other things. At first, I used a little cassette recorder and it was not too bad, but I found a good deal on a reel-to-reel recorder and it was much better. Unfortunately, I was not very happy with what I heard on the recordings, so I eventually obtained a reverb unit to make my voice sound more like I was in a church, rather than a living room. It helped, but I still didn't like certain parts of my vocals. Since my wife went to bed a few hours before me (she had to get up very early and I did not), I used my evenings to practice and improve. I also bought some background tracks and began using them. After weeks of trial and error, I started to get better vocal sounds. I changed the way I was forming vowels and phrasing in my songs and I began to produce whole songs that sounded the way I wanted them to. One morning, as I headed out to go to work, I was singing some lines from a song I had practiced the night before and while doing that, I started to do some ad-lib. I went up to some higher notes and did some little trills, to just play around with how the song would sound if I sang it that way. Within a few minutes, I stopped and said to myself, "Huh. I was never able to do that before." I knew that something had happened to my voice, as well as my skill. The hours of practice gave me vocal dexterity and strength that I never had before. My range was increased and my tones were so much different. I was thrilled. I also realized that God led me through the whole vocal training process so I could minister to people for him. During that whole time, I felt God around me and helping me. When I sang, I often felt him there with me.

During this same period, I recorded some songs and gave them to my mother. She was thrilled. To make a long story shorter, even before my voice was fully developed, I started getting invitations to sing more and more. The better I got, the more opportunities came my way. Soon, I was hired for retreats, weddings, funerals, and banquets. I was even asked to lead worship music for different organizations. So I crossed over from being an amateur to a professional vocalist in a fairly short period. Because people were asking me if I had any music albums, I started recording at a local studio and produced my first album. A few years later, I started booking full-time work and traveled as "The Singing Evangelist." In the years that followed, I ministered in well over 300 churches throughout the northwestern states and Canada. I also got the privilege of ministering several times on the live Praise the Lord Program (TBN) in Seattle, and on other Christian programs in the northwest and Alaska. Once I was able to get on a broadcast that reached eastern Russia.

For me, Christian music ministry is very important. People can often be moved in ways that words alone cannot do. Perhaps this is why we have 150 songs (Psalms) in our Bible. There is also the Song of Solomon, but it seems to be more about a Godly love between man and wife - though it can also be viewed as a parallel of the intimate relationship we have with God. Because these songs are in the Bible, we eventually need to read them. They have value – even prophetically. So, come with me, and let's explore the best way to study them.

Who to and Why?

Most Christians today, believe that all 150 Psalms were written for them; that is, directed to them. However, if we are going to be completely realistic about Bible study and see the purest truth of it, we need to know who the Psalms were written for. As a preface to that, I think we first need to see who wrote the Psalms. Now, some people seem to say that King David wrote the Psalms, but he did not write all of them. He did write about half of them, though. Somewhere between 70 and 80 have been credited to him. The other writers include Moses, Heman the Ezrahite, Ethan the Ezrahite, Solomon, Asaph, and the sons of Korah. So, what does this mean to us? Well, I think the most important thing to realize is that Psalms is a collection of music that was written over many years. In fact, the period between one of the first music authors (Moses) and one of the last (King Solomon) was well over 500 years. So, this music, or actually the lyrics for the music, was collected, one song at a time, and kept for use.

Now, let's stop and think about this. If the Israelites gathered music for hundreds of years, who do you think they were originally written for? Someone in New York City, in the years 2000, 2025, or 2050? I doubt they had that in mind when they were written since New York did not exist. I think it is pretty obvious that the Israelites wrote these songs for the Israelites. There seems to be no record of the Israelites publishing and distributing these songs to neighboring countries. I doubt any other countries would have sung these songs anyway since they talk about the God of Israel.

I am not sure that we have fully answered the question of why they were written, so let's explore that. If we look at the content of the Psalms, we can see that it is partitioned into five sections (though some scholars break it into eight sections). Across these sections, we may see themes like these:

- God the Creator.
- God the Redeemer.
- God the Judge.
- God's Glory.
- God's Sovereignty.
- God's Wisdom.
- God's Law.
- God's Mercy.
- The Incarnation.
- The Passion.
- The Church.
- Worship.
- Thanksgiving.
- Prayer.
- Trust in God.
- God our Refuge.
- Divine Guidance.
- In Time of Trouble.
- Righteousness.
- Peace.
- The Transitory Aspect of Life.
- The Hope of Immortality.
- Penitential Psalms.

We need to always remember that these are songs or at least poetic verses. The original song author likely sang what he wrote. We also see what appears to be clues about how some of the Psalms are to be sung. So, at least some of the Psalms were sung by groups. Many of the Psalms may have been used in group worship at the Temple.

When we look at the themes and content of the Psalms, we can relate to some of the things the Psalmists were feeling. Thus, it seems appropriate to empathize with the author and sing along with him (though we do not know the original tune). We serve the same God, so if the Psalmists were happy and praising God, we can voice the same thing. If we are sad and it feels like our enemies are gaining ground against us, we may relate to some of the Psalms where the author was concerned about similar circumstances.

So, is there value in reading the Psalms? Yes. We just need to remember that we are relating to the music author's situation, and not receiving all of the Psalms as a direction to our personal life. Yes, the Holy Spirit can pull out one of the Psalms and encourage us or give us direction, but this is a special circumstance and it is a divine miracle. In contrast, when we are just reading through Psalms, it would be wrong to take every single Psalm as a personal directive for our life. In case you have not read the entire Book of Psalms lately, let me tell you that many of the Psalms are depressing. The music author is pouring out his heartfelt sadness and internal struggles. So be careful how you read Psalms and remember how the Psalms were collected, and who the songs were originally meant for. Then, pray that God guides you through them, so you can glean the most from the collection of songs.

Time to Go to Work

Now that we have covered what Psalms is about, and what it is not, let's look at some sample passages.

Psalms 6: - 6 I am worn out from my groaning. All night long I flood my bed with weeping and drench my couch with tears. 7 My eyes grow weak with sorrow; they fail because of all my foes. 8 Away from me, all you who do evil, for the Lord has heard my weeping. 9 The Lord has heard my cry for mercy; the Lord accepts my prayer. 10 All my enemies will be overwhelmed with shame and anguish; they will turn back and suddenly be put to shame.

So, what do you get from this, when you read it as if you had never seen it before? It seems to me the songwriter is extremely sad and that this sadness may be caused by evil people. In contrast, he seems to know that God has heard his cry for help and will bring it. He is confident that his enemies will be dealt with. Now, what did you see in this portion of Psalms 6?

This seems like a typical format for many Psalms. It lays out a problem, and then by the end of the song, there is trust that God will deliver the person from the situation they are in. In most of the Psalms, there is a glimmer of hope, even in the worst situations. So, if we can weather (in some cases), many verses that state how bad a situation is, we will see the songwriter calling on God and trusting him. Perhaps this is why people with deep problems in their lives cling to the Psalms. They can relate to the flavor of despair in many of the Psalms, and see that it is not the end of the story.

Let's look at a different kind of Psalm:

Psalms 35: - 4 May those who seek my life be disgraced and put to shame; may those who plot my ruin be turned back in dismay. 5 May they be like chaff before the wind, with the angel of the Lord driving them away; 6 may their path be dark and slippery, with the angel of the Lord pursuing them. 7 Since they hid their net for me without cause and without cause dug a pit for me, 8 may ruin overtake them by surprise - may the net they hid entangle them, may they fall into the pit, to their ruin.

When I read this passage, I just have to say, wow. This sounds like a curse to me. What do you think? I thought the Psalms were supposed to be encouraging and uplifting. Can you imagine singing this song on Sunday morning in your church?

Now, it seems the language is pretty straightforward, so if we read this passage like we had never seen it and do not try to spiritualize it, I think we can easily get where the songwriter is going. Of course, when it comes to any song, whether written 3000 years ago or yesterday, we have to allow for "artistic flair." The music author in the Psalm may have wanted to rhyme words or match a specific music pattern. Additionally, he may have wanted to bring more attention to specific aspects, and in doing so, he may have used more colorful or flowery words than in normal speech. This tends to make song words more metaphoric. What we want to do is recognize these metaphoric tendencies in songs and not try to take them to the next level of over-spiritualizing them. Not everything the

Psalmists wrote has a dual meaning that echoed in the heavens or was part of a heavenly event. So, be careful.

Since it does not seem that there are odd phrases in this passage, we do not likely need huge searches for a word or phrase meanings. However, things that may be cultural and time-sensitive, may present difficulties for some readers. Let me point out a few of these. In the fifth verse, there is a mention of chaff. Some readers may not know what chaff is if they have no farming knowledge. Chaff is what is left over when the grain is removed from the stalk it grows on. Only the grain is needed, so the shell that was around the grain and the stock portion are thrown away. Historically, the chaff is usually put back into the soil or burned.

I think we understand the idea of a dark and slippery path (vs 6). I see the enemy likely falling, as the Lord is pursuing them. And, it sounds like the music author felt he had been trapped by his enemy without any cause. He is wishing the same thing would happen to his enemies. So, in a rightful sense, under the Law, it would be an "eye for an eye and a tooth for a tooth." Again, this seems brutal, but this was not an era of grace. It was an era of harsh and swift justice.

Before we leave the book of Psalms, let's explore the first part of Psalms 89. It was authored by Ethan the Ezrahite, not David, and yet it talks about David's family.

> **Psalm 89:1-4 --- I will sing of the Lord's great love forever; with my mouth I will make your faithfulness known through all generations. 2 I will declare that your love stands firm forever, that you have established your**

faithfulness in heaven itself. 3 You said, "I have made a covenant with my chosen one, I have sworn to David my servant, 4 'I will establish your line forever and make your throne firm through all generations.'

As you read this for the "first" time, what is your impression? It is a pretty great song, right? This is high praise. We could take this and use it as loud energetic praise in church on Sunday morning, right?

Besides its song and idea value, one important thing is that it is prophetic. Look at the third and fourth verses. The music author is quoting God and saying that he has made a contract with his chosen one. Now, this might sound a little odd to some readers, so we need to find out who this "chosen one" is. There might be some cross-references for this verse, but let's first take a more pure approach. Let's do a digital search for this phrase, using the entire Bible as the parameter. Go ahead, I will wait (doo, doo, doo … twiddle my thumbs). Okay, what did you find? When I searched, the results showed that the first time this phrase was used, it was referring to the king of Israel – namely Saul (2 Samuel 21:6). So does this Psalm seem to be talking about King Saul? No. It appears that the "chosen one" has to do with another king of Israel, David. God is quoted as having said that he would make a bloodline from King David that would not end. Not only would David's family bloodline not end, but his family line would be on the throne for all generations – in other words, forever.

If you are reading this Psalm similarly to the way I am, then you may have some questions. My first question is this: How can this be true? David's bloodline did not stay in power and on the throne forever. The whole nation of Israel (and after the split, Judah), was basically obliterated. There were thousands of years when there was no king at all. So, was the songwriter, wrong? Did he lie? If he did, then we need to throw down our Bible and declare that it is a false document and worthy of destruction.   But, did this music author truly lie? No. He had to have been moved by the Spirit of God to write this Psalm because it was a prophecy of the coming Messiah. And all who heard this song knew what the writer meant. The Messiah, the savior of the world was going to come from David's lineage and this Messiah was going to be a powerful king that would rule forever. What we know now, from things that Jesus said, is that he was the promised and chosen one. And, that the only way this prophecy could have ever been fulfilled, is if the Messiah could live forever, and retain his power eternally. We know now that only someone immortal could fulfill this prophecy and that he would need divine power to maintain the authority – to be able to stay on the throne forever. This is also backed by most commentaries that say Psalms 89 is talking about the coming Messiah.

Last Thoughts about Psalms

My impression of the Psalms is that they mainly contain petitions to the Lord, and praise for who he is, as well as what he has done. Mixed into these praises are looks into the future of Israel, and foretelling of the coming Messiah. When we are studying the Psalms, it is easy to get embroiled in alternate and symbolic meanings. However, it is very important that we first read just what is on the page and get the most out of the plain content of the words. If we can first get the overall subject and context of what the songwriter was saying, then we are much less likely to assign meaning that was not intended. Why am I so concerned about this? Because especially in the la la land of Eschatology (end times), scholars will pull any text that has metaphoric meaning and claim it means what they want it to say. When they connect it with other many other texts, it facilitates building what I call a "house of cards." This is not good Bible study, nor is it a good way to make or support doctrine. So, please, when you are reading any part of the Bible, try not to insert or connect ideas that are not clearly there.

Just because you can create a logical argument, does not mean it is what the original writers intended. And, just because you can quote two verses and come up with a belief that sounds good, does not mean it is proper Biblical doctrine. Perhaps doctrine should be handled less like a math equation, and more like chemistry. Most of us know that two atoms of Oxygen and one of Hydrogen, when combined, will make one molecule of water. However, water does not look like or act like either Oxygen or Hydrogen. Both these gases are flammable or greatly aid in the flammability of other materials, whereas water does neither. So …

We may be able to put Bible texts together and create something that sounds and looks wonderful, but the result may not have the same characteristics as the verses used.

Chapter 7

Prophets and Onions

Are prophets like onions? Do their prophecies have layers of meaning? Hmm. Maybe, maybe not. Okay, yes, I think this idea may have come from an old movie, but when we are reading the Bible, the Old Testament's foretelling of events that were to happen in Israel's future can be pretty confusing. So in this section, I want to see if we can pierce through some of the confusion and make sense of some very metaphoric and symbolic texts.

Backward Engineering

When I was a fairly new employee at a fabrication company, I was kind of "thrown under the bus." I suppose it was a kind of initiation or test of my skills, but it ended up being a little nightmare. Here is what happened: I was shown a metal box that had been made many years before and had several functions. I was told to identify all the parts, have them ordered, and make a copy of the box (yes, it was legal). At first, it was not very clear how to open the box, but once I got it open, I looked inside, and mostly what I saw was a massive amount of wires, going everywhere. My first impression, was, yikes! I expected more of a neat layout of the wiring and more of a clear view of the actual components. You see, the problem with all those wires being run randomly is that they blocked the view of everything that was behind them. With this rather sloppy approach to its build, the job of identifying parts was much more difficult.

At this point, I want to make a point about my skills. I had years of experience in repairing electrical and electronic circuits, and I was very good at understanding and repairing mechanical devices. I also had many years of practice in what is called "backward engineering." So, though this project was challenging, I did have the experience to do the job and do it well.

Okay, back to the project. I dove into the project and began writing down part numbers. When I had a list of the ones I could identity, I started looking the parts up on the internet to find sources where they could be procured. This is where the second stage of the nightmare began. Many of the parts were obsolete and others were special order – which meant long-lead times. My boss wanted this job done within a month or less. Here was another, yikes. I did the best I could to find alternate parts, but some parts were so special that we just could not substitute them. This was not good for our customers. Of course, this project had been in the queue long before I was employed, and everyone just kept throwing it aside, thinking it was going to be easy. Well, it was not, and the biggest challenge this box had was that it had to be outside and in any kind of nasty weather. Yeah, you got it: Electrical components in the rain. Not good. In the end, we did get the job done, but it was a lot more complex to copy and build than anyone had imagined. The company was way late in the deliveries, and it was, as I said, just a nightmare.

So, why tell you about a highly technical project, when many readers are not in technical professions? Well, it is like this: I wanted you to experience some of the frustration of complex situations where the details are not necessarily understood because it applies to unraveling prophetic texts. Looking into the OT prophecies is a lot like me looking into that equipment box and seeing a massive amount of wires, going in all directions. Our first impulse is to close the box (or close the Bible) and say, "Forget it." But let me tell you a little secret. If you sort of ignore the "forest" and just look at one "tree," you can make sense of it. When it comes to wires, all those bundles going everywhere are the forest and each wire is like an individual tree. When you find one wire and follow it, you can discover where it goes. Then you can have an "aha," moment where you can say, "Oh, that is how this one thing is connected to this other thing." If you are persistent and patient, you can trace each wire out and find out what connects to what. And, if you draw those connections on a note pad, you can get an idea of how the whole thing works (that is, if you have experience with those kinds of devices). The Bible works in much the same way. If we look at a whole book, or even a whole chapter, and try to make sense of the detailed text, we will run away in frustration – or we will start assigning meaning that is not there. Like a maze of wires, the only way to make sense of it is to explore it one wire at a time. So what are these "wires" in prophecy? Well, they are individual ideas. They are words and phrases. A single small idea can span one phrase, a whole verse, or several verses. This is a little like tracing wires: Some are big, and some are small. Some are long and some are short. But success is only realized when you look at just one wire and understand what that one wire is about. The same with prophetic information. Seeing the simple and single idea first is extremely important. Once you have the simple ideas understood, then later, you may be able to connect these ideas and see the bigger, picture. If the ideas are built correctly, without manipulating the text or imposing your own ideas, then you should be closer to what the writer intended.

Let me make another comparison with the box I was trying to copy. Everyone thought it was no big deal. They looked at the box and its function and said, that couldn't be hard. Many of the company's administrators already had planned out how the project would probably go. Without really looking at what was inside the box and how complex it was, they judged it on many assumptions. In a sense, they saw the forest and decided what probably made up that forest, but inside that forest were trees and vegetation that were rare and some were even extinct. If they had taken the time to look at each component that made up that forest, then they would have truly understood the forest. Today, there are way too many scholars who want to look at the forest of prophecy and make way too many assumptions. They tend to formulate a theme (doctrine), and then they try to squeeze the meaning of every verse into the mold. This is just plain bad Eschatology and bad Bible study.

This is one of the strongest themes of my book:

**When you read the Bible, do not take ideas
with you. Let the Bible give you the ideas.**

We can misunderstand so many things in the Bible when we put our ideas first. When we make the Bible say what we want it to say, then claim that our interpretation is nothing less than absolute truth – or even from the very mouth of God himself, we are in a dangerous place. The Bible should never be our version, backed by God. It is God who orchestrated the Bible, and we should always, every day, be looking to make sure that what he said is what we believe. And, just as many wall clocks need to be checked frequently to make sure they are telling the right time, we need to check our doctrine frequently, to make sure we are staying in line with what the Bible says – not what we want it to say. When the Bible comes in conflict with what we believe, then we change what we believe; we do not manipulate the Bible or try to explain it away, so we can keep our beliefs. When we change the meaning of God's Word to suit our views, then we are not following God, we are following our imaginations.

Work Time

Well, it is time to pick up your best reading glasses, a digital version of the Bible, and any other study tools you like. We are going to embark on a journey through some interesting scripture and some tough ones, to demonstrate how prophecies can be peeled back.

Let's start with one of the easier prophecies. It is one that was fulfilled thousands of years ago, and at the time of Jacob (Abraham's grandson). This is about Jacob's family, especially his youngest son, Joseph.

> **Genesis 37: - 5 Joseph had a dream, and when he told it to his brothers, they hated him all the more. 6 He said to them, "Listen to this dream I had: 7 We were binding sheaves of grain out in the field when suddenly my sheaf rose and stood upright, while your sheaves gathered around mine and bowed down to it." 8 His brothers said to him, "Do you intend to reign over us? Will you actually rule us?" And they hated him all the more because of his dream and what he had said. 9 Then he had another dream, and he told it to his brothers. "Listen," he said, "I had another dream, and this time the sun and moon and eleven stars were bowing down to me." 10 When he told his father as well as his brothers, his father rebuked him and said, "What is this dream you had? Will your mother and I and your brothers actually come and bow down to the ground before you?" 11 His brothers were jealous of him, but his father kept the matter in mind.**

Now, before you listen to my ramblings, first try to harvest your own ideas about what this passage is saying. Take it for its surface value, without going into any deep meanings. What does the text say, what does it not say? When you have finished reading it a couple of times, then you can read what I think.

What I see here is that Joseph's brothers already hated him, before he had any dreams. So we need to be clear that these dreams were not the original cause of the sibling rivalry. If you read the verses before this passage, you will see that Jacob favored Joseph, and he did special things for Joseph that he did not do for his other sons. I would say, if this was today, that this is bad parenting - but rather than judge that aspect, let's look at what happens just within this text. Joseph has a dream and in it, he is with his brothers in a field and they are all tying harvested grain into bundles. Suddenly, one of the bundles that Joseph had tied, rose from its laid-down position and stood upright. The bundles of grain that his brothers tied, gathered around Joseph's upright bundle, and bowed down to it. Now, when Joseph told his brothers about his dream, they interpreted his dream as Joseph becoming someone important and them serving him. This idea caused them to hate him even more.

As if this was not bad enough, Joseph had another dream and again, he told his brothers - as well as his father. This time, the sun, moon, and eleven stars (the number of his brothers) bowed down to Joseph. This dream seems a little more obvious, since Joseph is actually in the dream, rather than him being represented by a symbol. But, what is the response of his father? He rebuked him. His dad asked, "Will your mother and I and your brothers actually come and bow down to the ground before you?"

It was obvious that neither his brothers nor his father believed that they would ever be subservient to the youngest boy, and yet if we read the rest of the story in Genesis, we see that Joseph did rise to power in Egypt and his whole family bowed before him. The odd thing about this is that the hateful actions of Joseph's brothers led to Joseph becoming a ruler over them. So, in a real fashion, Joseph's brothers "shot themselves in the foot." Their own stupid jealously became the very path for Joseph to be exalted. Perhaps there is a lesson for us here? Trying to destroy someone may not work out the way you think. You may end up helping them to a better place. This seems to be part of God's grace and justice being in perfect balance.

Let's look again at this prophetic dream. So many prophecies in the Old Testament are taken and twisted so they can be applied to the twenty-first-century church, and I am sure someone has used this one for those means also. But, the meaning of the dreams was clear to Joseph's family and they considered it just for them. Perhaps God revealed the meaning to them, but either way, it was not a mystery. They did not call on a wise man, or a prophet of God to come and interpret the dream. They knew, and they stated it. Within the same Bible book, this prophecy was fulfilled. So, the ideas surrounding this dream and its climax are given in scripture. End of story. So, it would not be proper to try to take this out of context and make it mean something else. And, we certainly should not import it into end-times doctrine. This dream is not – I repeat - not about anything but Joseph rising to power and his family being under his rule. At least this is the way I see it. Of course, you may get something else and as long as you do not impose ideas on this text, your opinion is as valid as mine. ☺

Before we leave this passage of scripture, let me point out one more thing. Notice the use of the symbols sun, moon, and stars. Now, this is a huge question: What does the text say these represent? The family knew what they stood for and Jacob voiced it to Joseph. These heavenly bodies symbolized Joseph's father, mother, and brothers. This is very important because these symbols in a prophecy did not represent the actual sun, moon, or stars – none of them. So, we need to be very careful when we read about dreams and prophecies that come later in the Bible. If the first time God used these symbols, they meant leaders or people of authority (mother and father, for instance), and siblings (family or tribe), then when we see these symbols in a later prophecy, we should not immediately assume that they are the physical sun, moon, and stars. In fact, it is more likely they represent people, authority, leaders, family, fellow countrymen, etc. So file this away in the back of your mind and when you read end-times prophecies, remember this early prophecy. It may have defined terms that were going to be used throughout the rest of the Bible.

When we consider prophetic dreams in the Bible, it is important to hear what God said about them. So, consider his words in the book of Numbers.

> **Numbers 12:6-8 --- "… he (God) said, "Listen to my words: "When there is a prophet among you, I, the Lord, reveal myself to them in visions, I speak to them in dreams. 7 But this is not true of my servant Moses; he is faithful in all my house. 8 With him I speak**

**face to face, clearly and not in riddles; he sees
the form of the Lord."**

I think the message is pretty clear here. If we believe what God has said, then we must believe that God gives prophetic dreams to the people he chooses. We also know that except for Moses, these dreams will not be clear. I am going to say this again and emphasize it. God said what he would speak in dreams to his prophets, would not be clear; it would be in "riddles." Thus, my encouragement to all end-times scholars is this: DO NOT TAKE THE CONTENT OF PROPHETIC DREAMS LITERALLY. This is a wrong interpretation of most or all prophetic dreams (or visions). If God said they are riddles, we need to take heed.

Next Example

Now, I am not going to lead you through a massive maze of OT prophecy. There is just not enough room in this book, and after all, this is about learning techniques, not creating a new Bible commentary.

Let's now consider one of the most mind-boggling prophetic books in the Bible, Isaiah. It is a book that is full of riddles. It may or may not be the most difficult to understand, but it contains the most chapters with riddles. Before we look at any verses, let me first give you an overview of this book. First, it cannot be read as a story. It is a collection of the prophecies that the prophet gave. These prophecies are not to one person or nation. Many of them are for the Children of Israel, but some are also for their rival nations, such as Babylon (modern-day Iraq), Assyria (parts of modern-day Turkey and Iraq),

Egypt, Arabia, and others. So when you read Isaiah, you need to consider each chapter separately. Each one stands alone and may or may not have anything to do with any other chapter. Also, within the many riddle-type prophecies in Isaiah, there are numerous references to the coming Messiah. Even these, however, are mixed in with other information. So, each prophecy is a tapestry of interwoven ideas. Where we sit, so many years after the prophecies, it is very hard to make sure of the meanings. However, do not give up. All is not lost. What we do know for sure are the things that God explains in the prophecies. He also does this in books like Daniel and Revelation. Many things are left as riddles, but some things are spelled out. There is another aspect to the book of Isaiah, also. Jesus and the Apostles quoted Isaiah to make certain points or show the fulfillment of scripture. So, we can take these New Testament references and at least partially interpret what Isaiah wrote. Also, when we look at historical events both in and out of the Bible, we may be able to see how some of the riddles played out in real life.

I think that is enough background for now, so let's look at a specific text.

Isaiah 6: - In the year that King Uzziah died, I saw the Lord, high and exalted, seated on a throne; and the train of his robe filled the temple. 2 Above him were seraphim, each with six wings: With two wings they covered their faces, with two they covered their feet, and with two they were flying. 3 And they were calling to one another: "Holy, holy, holy is the Lord Almighty; the whole earth is full

**of his glory." 4 At the sound of their voices
the doorposts and thresholds shook and the
temple was filled with smoke. 5 "Woe to
me!" I cried. "I am ruined! For I am a man
of unclean lips, and I live among a people of
unclean lips, and my eyes have seen the King,
the Lord Almighty." 6 Then one of the
seraphim flew to me with a live coal in his
hand, which he had taken with tongs from
the altar. 7 With it he touched my mouth
and said, "See, this has touched your lips;
your guilt is taken away and your sin atoned
for." 8 Then I heard the voice of the Lord
saying, "Whom shall I send? And who will go
for us?" And I said, "Here am I. Send me!" 9
He said, "Go and tell this people: 'Be ever
hearing, but never understanding; be ever
seeing, but never perceiving.' 10 Make the
heart of this people calloused; make their
ears dull and close their eyes. Otherwise they
might see with their eyes, hear with their
ears, understand with their hearts, and turn
and be healed."**

Okay, now, go back and read this passage again, and make sure
you do not put in any of your own fill-ins. Now after looking
at it carefully, what did you read? What did the words say and
what did they not say? Make up your mind before you
consider anything I say. Here is what I see: The first
important thing about this passage is the question of when the
prophecy was given. This is important because it tells us who
it was for. It was primarily a message to the people who lived

in the year after King Uzziah died. Now, who was King Uzziah? Well, at this point, I am not going to look that up for you. If you do a digital search in the Bible, you will see all the references to King Uzziah. I will give you a hint, though. All the records of the kings of Israel and Judah are within four OT books that are grouped. Okay, so now that we know the timeframe, the next important thing to note is that Isaiah is being shown a vision/dream. God is not dictating a description of things to Isaiah, he is showing Isaiah images. He sees the Lord (or an image that represents the Lord), his throne, and more. There are angels around the throne area and they are giving the Lord praise. Isaiah sees all this and he suddenly realizes he is very "dirty" (possibly in comparison to God). Isaiah's guilt is taken away when an angel takes a live coal from the altar and touches Isaiah's lips. Now, this is very interesting, because the angel is handling the live coal with tongues, yet there is no indication that Isaiah was burned by it or hurt in any way. It seems more like he received a kind of healing from the burning coal. Of course, this was spiritual healing of Isaiah's sin, not physical. In this portion of the riddle, I think we can fairly safely say, that this live coal was symbolic. Since it did not burn, then it is unlikely that it had any physical heat. Now we can stop and make all kinds of connections to Christ's atonement and the temple's altar, etc., but let's not. When we start making connections that the scriptures do not specifically call out, we start down a slippery slope. We can muse about the possibility of connections, and even be amazed at the possibilities, but if the Bible does not specifically make these connections or definitions, then we should be very careful about assigning meaning that is not actually written on the page or referenced elsewhere in God's Word.

The next thing I see is the Lord talking to Isaiah. He is asking, who will go (as a messenger, I assume). Then someone undefined says, I will go. So, God says to this volunteer to go and tell the Children of Israel this: "Be ever hearing, but never understanding; be ever seeing, but never perceiving." Now, we might ask "why" at this point, and God does answer this question. He follows up by saying this: "Make the heart of this people calloused; make their ears dull and close their eyes. Otherwise they might see with their eyes, hear with their ears, understand with their hearts, and turn and be healed." A pretty odd statement isn't it? It sounds like God intends to purposely harden their hearts and hide the truth from them. Does this sound fair? No. But, these last two verses were quoted in all four of the Gospel books in the New Testament (Matt. 13:14-15; Mark 4:11-12; Luke 8:10; John 12:40), so they must be a critical element of God's plan. Paul even quotes this in Acts 28:26-27. Now, how do I know this? By using RID. This text in Isaiah sounded odd, so I did a digital search for some of the used phrases in the Bible. What I found included NT verses where Jesus and others quoted this passage in Isaiah. It was such a simple process and it took only a couple of minutes but blew open a door to so much more clarity for this passage. We did not need to invent clever theories or fill in the text with our musings. We found the actual words of our Savior, telling us how this played in real-time.

Let's look at one of these texts in the NT and see how this prophecy unfolds.

> **Matthew 13: - 10 The disciples came to him and asked, "Why do you speak to the people in parables?" 11 He replied, "Because the**

**knowledge of the secrets of the kingdom of
heaven has been given to you, but not to
them. 12 Whoever has will be given more,
and they will have an abundance. Whoever
does not have, even what they have will be
taken from them. 13 This is why I speak to
them in parables: "Though seeing, they do
not see; though hearing, they do not hear or
understand. 14 In them is fulfilled the
prophecy of Isaiah: You will be ever hearing
but never understanding; you will be ever
seeing but never perceiving. 15 For this
people's heart has become calloused; they
hardly hear with their ears, and they have
closed their eyes. Otherwise they might see
with their eyes, hear with their ears,
understand with their hearts and turn, and I
would heal them.**

In this passage of scripture, we are told why Jesus taught in
riddles (parables). It sounds like the people in his day (the
same as in Isaiah's day) were rebellious and did not want to
follow God with all their hearts. They refused to receive Jesus'
message. The real kicker is that Jesus saw this and knew ahead
of time that they would not receive his message. God knew in
Isaiah's day, that the people in Jesus' time would not receive
his message. So what did God do? What did Jesus do? They
veiled the truth in riddles. But, why? Because Jesus said
"Whoever has will be given more, and they will have an
abundance. Whoever does not have, even what they have will
be taken from them." What can this mean? Well, I will let you
make up your own mind, but I remember that Jesus said

everyone is given a measure of faith. So everyone has a little something to start with in the beginning. If each Jewish person was given enough in the beginning, but many of them refused to take up that faith and use it, then it was taken away. Those who kept their faith and used it were given more information, so they could take the next step in faith toward God. Now, I might be going out on a limb here, but it seems to me by this scripture (and others covering this idea) that Jesus did not want to add more sin and guilt on those who he knew would refuse his message. Jesus knew they were already condemned. They had already built up a pile of sins and wrongdoing. Out of compassion, Jesus (as his Father also had done), kept information from them, so he would not add to their guilt. If he had spoken plainly, and then they rejected the message, they would have deserved and gotten a greater punishment. Jesus did not want to be responsible for adding to the misery of his fellow countrymen. Now, this is what I see as his motive, but you can draw your conclusions.

Wrap

You can see the connection between Jesus' ministry and the referenced prophecy in Isaiah. This makes it much easier to interpret that one portion of Isaiah chapter 6 (verses 9 & 10). In fact, like a puzzle, once we have that piece in place, we may be able to properly decipher at least some of the text around the 9th and 10th verses. However, just because we may be able to expand a little on the part we know, does not mean we will perfectly interpret all the other surrounding riddles in the sixth chapter or the other chapters of Isaiah. To truly and properly divide those words, we need other quotes from Jesus or his followers – and there are some others. Go, search, find and explore. You will find it time-consuming, but fascinating, when you unlock some of the prophetic mysteries just by simple word/phrase searches and cross-references.

Chapter 8

How Clear are the Gospels?

I received my first full Bible when I was quite young. It was a black leather-bound version that included a zipper. The zipper was nice because it would not flop open when you didn't want it to, and the pages did not get wet when I had to dash through the rain. When I entered Junior High School, I began to carry my Bible every day. The zip-up version became very handy when I carried it with all my other books - and when considering the distance I had to walk to school. So I thank my parents for their wise forethought, and I thank my Lord that he was watching out for me.

When I first received my Bible and began reading it, I had no thought about whether it was accurate or infallible. I accepted it as a book that told me about Jesus and how to live as a Christian. And, you know what? It did that very well. Yes, I know that many theologians and learned scholars can get all uppity and technical about the Bible, then become sort of "god-like," in their dominating claims concerning it, but the message our Bible contains, seems to be the real reason the Bible exists.

Is the Bible infallible? We explored the answer to this question in the early part of this book, but as a quick review, let me repeat some things. First of all, the experts will never stop debating this - and each of them has their own ideas. Many say that the original text was flawless and exactly the way God authored it. Others say that the King James Bible is a proper translation and it is flawless. The idea that our Bible could have any error is abhorrent to us, and yet we know that all translations are dependent on the manuscripts they were translated from. The problem scholars have is that the ancient manuscripts and pieces of manuscripts do not all agree. Today we have over 5000 documents (some are fragments) to reference when looking for the most accurate manuscript. Kind of a nightmare, right? Well, though it has been a challenge to Biblical purists, experts have been through them all and made good judgments about how to use them. Whole groups of good men and women and gone over them thoroughly, and guess what they discovered? In a worst-case scenario, there is only about a 1% difference between all those 5000 pieces. And, why is this amazing? Because they were all copied by hand (not printed). The second amazing thing is that none of these differences affect fundamental Christian doctrine. Jesus is still Lord and Savior. He is still born of a virgin and the Son of the Living God. He still died on the cross to save us and offers salvation out of his grace, when we accept his terms, through faith in Him.

Perhaps the infallibility of the Bible is something only God can judge. Whether we consider the Bible we hold in our hand, to be without flaw or not, we can rightfully say that there are viable questions about how it compares to the first version. This is because no one has the very first version of the Bible. Those documents could not be preserved. Thus, the best and oldest versions of the Bible texts are still copies. The question we should be asking is not about the perfection of the text. It is about the accuracy of its content. Let me demonstrate. I was a technical writer by trade, for about 15 years. During that time, I had to take the information from one source, glean its content, and write it in different words. However, after it was rewritten, it had to still contain accurate technical information. Just because the approach or explanation was different, the accuracy of the content had to be spot on. So, I know from experience that we can all say things differently, but still communicate the same ideas.

When we look at the Bible, one of the most important things to consider is how the information got from God, through men, and onto a written page. One thing we know for sure is that God did not sit down with a pen and write it. The only things God is recorded as having written (in stone or on walls), were copied to a page by a human being. This in itself introduces a margin of error. However, when we have different people writing the same ideas over centuries, and it ties into real-life facts, then we know there is a force that is larger and more powerful than men, right? So, we know that in some way, God was directing the content of the writing.

Let's turn up the power of our microscope, now and look a little more closely at the process of Bible writing. A very important factor is that people wrote Biblical content for different reasons. Several books in the Bible have great lessons and show us how God worked with human beings, yet the way they are written is very historical in approach. They are formulated as much as a history book as they are a book about Spiritual things. So, it appears that many books were written for posterity. The writers wanted the following generations to know what had happened. Much of the reasoning was that generations of people who did not see God perform fantastic miracles would believe in him and serve him. The importance of this was grave because if the future Children of Israel did not follow God, there were dire consequences.

Other aspects we need to consider in Bible writings are prophecies. There are a lot of words that were spoken by men that God chose. Prophets like Moses, Elijah, Elisha, Isaiah, Jeremiah, Ezekiel, Daniel, and many more, were God's spokesmen. And, not only did they audibly speak God's message, but some also wrote them down (or had them written). This brings up another issue. Did God sit down in the prophet's living room and tell him what to say and write? Well, no. Of course, it might have been on a mountaintop, in the desert, or maybe even at the home of the prophet, but the location is not so important. It is the manner. At times God sent an angel to the prophet. Other times, God just seemed to talk directly to them. With Moses, of course, he talked plainly, face to face. However, there were also several times that prophets received dreams or visions. God explained some things that the prophets were shown, but not all of them. So imagine this: You are a prophet of God. In the night you have a dream and you know it is from God and it is about the future of your country. When you wake up, you go to your papyrus scroll and begin writing with a quill pen. Your task is to accurately remember everything that you saw and heard.

God's Spirit is with you as you write, to make sure what you write is accurate, but he is not dictating it to you. So, you are relaying your experience in your words. If we stop and think about this for a minute, we can see that if two prophets were shown the same thing that night and they both wrote everything down, the content would be the same, but the two versions would not be exact copies. Now, yes, I know some scholars who might claim that they would be the same. I am going to say, they would not. Over millennia, God has spoken in many different ways, through men, and God has shown over and over that he allows people to express what God has told them, in their own terms – as long as it was correct. Every "the", "and, or "but", did not have to be by God's divine intervention. It was not necessary. Apparently, God likes it when people talk to other people with common terms. If some of you readers are skeptical at this point, let's consider what Paul said about the gifts of the Spirit. There is not a lot of difference (if any), between God's Spirit coming on an OT prophet and speaking through him or having him write things down – and the Holy Spirit coming on a Believer to speak a word of prophecy, wisdom, or knowledge in the early church. It is the same work of our Lord, done in a slightly different way. So let's consider this passage about Spiritual gifts.

> **1 Corinthians 14: - 26 What then shall we say, brothers and sisters? When you come together, each of you has a hymn, or a word of instruction, a revelation, a tongue or an interpretation. Everything must be done so that the church may be built up. 27 If anyone speaks in a tongue, two—or at the most three—should speak, one at a time, and**

**someone must interpret. 28 If there is no
interpreter, the speaker should keep quiet in
the church and speak to himself and to God.
29 Two or three prophets should speak, and
the others should weigh carefully what is
said. 30 And if a revelation comes to
someone who is sitting down, the first
speaker should stop. 31 For you can all
prophesy in turn so that everyone may be
instructed and encouraged. 32 The spirits of
prophets are subject to the control of
prophets.**

We can see by this letter Paul wrote to the Corinthian church,
that a person who is under the power of God to speak his
Word, is also fully in control of himself and that the gift that is
given to speak a public message from God is subject to the
vessel that is used. Thus if a prophet is given a word, the
message he speaks will be God's message, but the phrasing
may be according to the vessel it goes through. Some people I
have met, tell me about things God has shown them. Often it is
a vision of objects or events. They tell in their words, what
God has shown them. God did not instruct them on exactly
how they were to describe what they saw. He depended on a
faithful follower of his to relay the message correctly. God did
not have to dictate the words. Before God ever chose that
person to give a dream or vision, God knew they were an
honorable vessel to use and that they would relay the vision
accurately. I see the prophets of the OT doing similar things.
They are shown or told things and then they relay them,
accurately, but they use the phrasing of their commonly spoken

language. Still what God has said; still accurate, just not dictated – inspired, but not dictated.

What about the Gospel Books?

When it comes to the four books of the Bible that are often called the "Gospel Books," (Matthew, Mark, Luke, and John) we would expect they would all be in harmony or even carbon copies of each other. I mean, after all, if God directed that each word and phrase be exactly from his mouth (that is, dictated), then wouldn't they all be the same or very close? Also, since these four books tell the most important story in the entire Bible, wouldn't God make sure they were flawlessly told? I would think so, yet again, what is our idea or definition or flawless? As I said, I was a technical writer for many years, and you know what many people do not know about technical writing? We do not write in proper English. We are not supposed to. Technical writing is about the clarity and accuracy of technical information. Each writer uses what they hear as common words and phrases. Each writer uses their judgment as to what that is, and it can change according to the regions where they live. No two technical writers will use the same words or phrases to communicate the required ideas - and yet, if the writer is doing their job correctly, the person reading the text will know exactly what to do and how to do it. So, just because a script reads differently, does not mean it is inaccurate. Two technical documents that cover the same instructions can be quite different, and yet both can be accurate and "flawless." One document may include details or extra information that the other one does not have. They are still accurate and considered to be without flaws.

If you have read the four Gospel books, you know that they are not the same. There are some interesting similarities in the way information is laid out in Matthew and Mark, and many scholars have speculated that Matthew used Mark's writing as a reference when he wrote the book of Matthew. It is possible, but it has no bearing on its genuine nature or its accuracy. Luke's writing includes many things that Matthew and Mark wrote, but he adds more detail in some places, and in other places, he does not include the same information. In other places, the order in which he presents Jesus' teachings or directives is a little different. So, scholars do not see Matthew or Mark's writings to be the main base for Luke's writing. I should probably note here that the first three Gospel books are often called the "synoptic" Gospels since they similarly cover the story of Jesus.

So, what about the book of John? Well, this seems quite puzzling at times. The Apostle John wrote this book in a much different fashion. It appears that he may relay Jesus' life and events in a non-linear way. Some things Jesus did (like the clearing of the Temple), seem to have happened toward the end of his life in the synoptic Gospels, and yet at least one of the events (clearing of the temple) is placed early in the book of John. Now, this event could have happened more than one time, but none of the four Gospel books suggest that it did. Also, oddly enough, John does not talk about Jesus' parables at all, and he says very little about the end times. Instead, John focuses on who Jesus was to the disciples and how he interacted with them. Because it is so personal, it has become one of the most powerful books in the Bible to bring people to Christ for salvation.

So, is the book of John accurate? Is it flawless? To answer this, we have to compare again to technical writing methods (for example). What is the information that is needed to complete the task properly? First, what is the task? Well, Jesus came to save that which was lost, right? So, our question must be this: Do all four Gospels serve to portray Jesus as someone who was trying to seek out the lost and bring them to (or back to) God? And is the information relayed in a way that allows us to follow Jesus' example (and his instructions)? I think most Christians would answer a resounding, yes! So, each of the four Gospel books (on their own) tells us the requirements of Jesus' task and our task. Lastly, what information is needed to complete the task properly? In other words, does the "how" to seek and save the lost appear in each of the Gospel books? Again, Christians will resoundingly say, yes. So, what can be our conclusion? It seems that we can rightfully say that though the Gospel books present different perspectives and details about Jesus and his disciples, they all have the correct information and they all instruct us accurately about the task that God gave Jesus, and us. They are accurate, and their information/instruction is not flawed. Because we see this harmony between the Gospel books, and in fact with all of the books in the New Testament that talk about Jesus, we can tell that God was directing the writers.

Clarity

One thing we have not covered is clarity. When we study the Gospel books, how clear is the text to us? It seems many things are clear about Jesus' life and his journeys, but what about what he taught? He used parables and these (Jesus said) were purposed to be riddles that would not be clear until much later. Most or all of these have been figured out, largely because Jesus did tell his disciples (only) what they meant. So even the parables should be pretty clear to us. Now, what about his "end-times" statements? Well, these too seemed to carry some mystery. His disciples did not fully understand what he said, but they remembered it, and when the time came for them to act, they responded and their lives were saved. Yes, I know there is immeasurable debate surrounding Jesus' return and when it happened or when it will happen, but there are some pretty clear statements that Jesus said to his disciples before he went to the cross and some he made at his trial.

Now, I don't want this book to be a discourse on Eschatology, so I am not going to present any of that here. I covered all that pretty thoroughly in my other two books, REVELATION WITHOUT INFLAMMATION, and JESUS' WORDS WITHOUT INFLAMMATION. These books go through New Testament prophetic scripture, using the RID method, to sort out fact from fiction. Their purpose is not to draw conclusions but to show how to look at end-times text without manipulating it. The idea is to look at what the text actually says and what it does not say.

Okay, back to clarity. There can be some things in the Gospel books that are very clear and some that are not. For a sampling of methodology, let's look at a couple of texts.

> **John 14:14 - You may ask me for anything in
> my name, and I will do it.**

Here is a quote from the book of John that has been badly misused. When we read just this verse, we can easily get the idea that God will give us everything we ask (no matter how inappropriate or selfish). However, this is not the context for Jesus' statement. Let's take a look at the surrounding text to see what Jesus is actually saying.

> **John 14: - 12 Very truly I tell you, whoever believes in me will do the works I have been doing, and they will do even greater things than these, because I am going to the Father. 13 And I will do whatever you ask in my name, so that the Father may be glorified in the Son. 14 You may ask me for anything in my name, and I will do it. 15 "If you love me, keep my commands."**

When you read this whole text, what do you see? You will need to draw your own conclusions first. Here is what I see simplistically: Jesus says (as a general statement) that whoever believes in him will do the works he had been doing (at this point, this was mostly the disciples and close followers). Does this mean that every believer will do all the miracles Jesus did? No, because Paul is clear that the Spirit gives gifts to do these things as He sees fit, and he does not give the same gifts to everyone. So, again, Jesus seems to be making a generalized statement about the believers as a whole body. After he says this, he immediately, and in the same flow of thought, says that they can ask anything in "Jesus' name" and he will honor their request. What does this mean? Well, we need to remember that the "name" of a person is their reputation, mannerism, and authority. So this would be asking for something and doing something in the place of Christ. In other words, a believer would be standing in the place of Christ, representing him and carrying his authority. This is the context of the "ask." Thus, if one of the disciples wanted a golden palace for themselves, they could not walk into the desert and say, I command this, or I ask this in Jesus' name, and poof, they would have a new place to live. No. This would not be in the character of Christ, and it was not part of their commission, as his representatives. Also notice verses 14 and 15, together as the same flow of thought: 14 "You may ask me for anything in my name, and I will do it. 15 "If you love me, keep my commands." Again, we see a reference back to their relationship and obligation to Christ. "If you love me …" So, in context, it seems Jesus has put some pretty strong stipulations on this "ask anything." It is an asking that has to do with things that carry on the work of Christ and fulfill their commission. It has nothing to do with selfish gain.

I hope that a Fresh Read of this text in John will give you some insight into what Jesus told his disciples about asking things of him. I also hope that you can see what Jesus did not say in this passage.

Now, does this text have any odd words or phrases that need defining? Hmm. Perhaps "in Jesus' name" could cause some concern, since we do not use this phrase in our culture. I think we have this idea today, but not in those terms. We can look up several other scriptures to see what this means and it may bring us better clarity. It may also be helpful to look this term up in a Bible Dictionary. The idea of this phrase is pretty simple, so even Bible Dictionaries will probably be pretty accurate. However, if you are doing your due diligence, you will search for other texts and see how the Dictionary definitions line up with the way the term "in Jesus' name" is used.

Is there anything that is not told or not easily definable in this passage of scripture? If so, leave it for now, and do not try to make up your own explanation. Let God be God.

Another Example

Let's move on to another example.

> **Matthew 8: - 14 When Jesus came into Peter's house, he saw Peter's mother-in-law lying in bed with a fever. 15 He touched her hand and the fever left her, and she got up and began to wait on him. 16 When evening came, many who were demon-possessed were brought to him, and he drove out the spirits with a word and healed all the sick. 17 This was to fulfill what was spoken through the prophet Isaiah: "He took up our infirmities and bore our diseases."**

When you take this in as a Fresh Read, what do you see? Without assigning any other ideas, songs, poems, or traditional phrases, what do you think this text is saying? And, what is it not saying? To me, the story part is pretty clear. Jesus goes to Peter's house and Peter's mother-in-law is sick. She is running a fever, but Jesus touches her hand and she immediately gets well (or at least the fever left and she regained her strength). She then gets up and serves Jesus' needs. While in the house, that evening, many other sick people were brought to Jesus for healing. Among the sick were also people who needed to be delivered from demonic possession. What is great, is that Jesus healed them all and drove out all the evil spirits.

In the last verse of this passage, there is a conclusion that is not part of the story. The writer connects a scripture from the book of Isaiah and claims that Jesus fulfilled this prophecy when he healed the sick and drove out the demons. So, when studying, what should we do about this connection to an OT prophecy? Well, an average Christian reader would likely just say, oh, that is nice; how wonderful and move on. However, if we truly want to see the full connection between what the writer was talking about, we need to know what this passage in Isaiah says. The writer is providing text, that to him and his fellow Jews is very familiar, but it may not be to us. If we take this referenced prophecy as a single verse, we can get the wrong idea. Now, we have done many word and phrase searches in the Bible, and we have shied away from connecting verses that the Bible writers did not specifically say were supposed to be connected – however, here we have a Bible writer specifically connecting one verse to another. So, we must make sure our Fresh Read includes all of what is being presented. We want to look at only the given text, but we want to make sure we get all of the given text. So, let's go see where this verse is in Isaiah.

Isaiah 53:4 – "Surely he took up our pain and bore our suffering ..."

So, what do you think? Does this say the same thing that the NT writer is claiming? I would say so, but let's look at a larger portion of this passage.

Isaiah 53: - Who has believed our message and to whom has the arm of the Lord been revealed? 2 He grew up before him like a tender shoot, and like a root out of dry ground. He had no beauty or majesty to attract us to him, nothing in his appearance that we should desire him. 3 He was despised and rejected by mankind, a man of suffering, and familiar with pain. Like one from whom people hide their faces he was despised, and we held him in low esteem. 4 Surely he took up our pain and bore our suffering, yet we considered him punished by God, stricken by him, and afflicted. 5 But he was pierced for our transgressions, he was crushed for our iniquities; the punishment that brought us peace was on him, and by his wounds we are healed.

Does seeing the whole passage change the meaning of the verse that was quoted in the New Testament? Does it broaden your scope of understanding or does it produce some questions? Hmm. When I read this, I think that it pretty obviously refers to the coming Messiah, Jesus. It also seems to focus mostly on Jesus' suffering and death on the cross. However, this is looking at it from the future, backward. It does not mention a cross or Calvary or Golgotha. There are no nails included, whippings, beatings, or crowns of thorns. So much of what we know about the suffering of Christ is not included in this text. Thus, unavoidably, we tend to read a lot into this prophecy. Perhaps we can do a simple analysis and see if it changes the meaning. First, I am not sure what the first verse means, but it seems to suggest that the prophecy may not be believed by most and that God's power has not been revealed to many – or perhaps they just do not believe what they see is from God. Of course, this is a loose interpretation and it could be quite flawed, so at this point, it is mostly speculation. Is this bad? Well, no, it is only bad if I start clinging to my speculation as doctrine. Sometimes all we can do is speculate because remember that prophecy is presented in a riddle format.

Next, we have a reference to a "he." Since we do not know who the "he" is, we hope the following text will give us some clues. Of course, unless this type of pronoun is identified, usually "he" in prophecy means God or the promised Messiah. Of course, you would need to do a fair amount of reading prophecies to see this pattern. Now, this second verse says the Messiah will grow up like a tender shoot and will be out of the dry ground. I suppose this could mean he didn't come from a rich, powerful, or royal family, but it is a riddle. This text also says he was not particularly handsome (probably also not tall or large in stature). So, contrary to what all our modern movies and artistry show, Jesus did not have that model look and he did not stand out in a crowd. Perhaps this served to help him not be identified by authorities. Physically, he was just a common-looking, plain man. At least that is what I get from this text. I could be wrong, of course. You see what you think.

The text that follows talks about the Messiah being despised and rejected; says he was a man of suffering and familiar with pain. Now, I think many Bible teachers want to assign this to Jesus' suffering on the cross, but I see this word, "familiar," and have to wonder if this is more about long-term suffering and pain. If he was rejected, day after day, as he ministered, it would be emotionally painful. So is this text about the cross? I would say, probably not. It could include Jesus' suffering on the cross, but that was for just one day. Jesus suffered abuse for years, long before he went to the cross. So, it seems the weight of this text, so far, is not about the Messiah's death.

Now, we are down to the text that was quoted: "Surely he took up our pain and bore our suffering …" Matthew is claiming this was fulfilled when Jesus healed the sick and drove out demons at Peter's house. So, is this passage about Jesus' crucifixion? It does not seem that way, but you be the judge. Of course, the first half of this verse in Isaiah could be misleading, so let's make sure we connect it with the whole verse: "Surely he took up our pain and bore our suffering, yet we considered him punished by God, stricken by him, and afflicted." Okay, now we see this in a different light – maybe. We see Isaiah saying that the Messiah took up our pain and suffering, yet, people thought that God abandoned him and punished him. This last part certainly seems to be about Christ's death, because Jesus was not physically stricken before that time. You can see now, why so many scholars want to connect Jesus' taking up our pain and suffering with the cross, only. And, yet when they do, they ignore the very plain and simple reference that Matthew included. So maybe some of the problems are in the way it is read. Here is where Fresh Read comes into play. Let's look at this whole verse again. Without manipulating it, what would it say if we read it in a novel and it had nothing to do with Jesus? In other words, what exactly are the phrasing and syntax? Let's dissect it.

1. Someone took our physical pain and suffering.

2. Even so, we all (or most of us), thought he was
   punished because he did something wrong.

This is pretty much the gist of what verse 4 says. So the first part of this says Jesus was so compassionate and caring, that he decided to pick up our pain, disease, and other suffering and carry it. The second part of the verse is a "however," not a continuation. We have this word, "yet" between the two parts of verse four that many scholars ignore. It is not rocket science – it is Fresh Read. If we read it the way we do any other literature, we see that it is a contrast between Christ's compassionate attitude toward people and their wrongful conclusion that God had rejected him and was punishing him for wrongdoing. So, let me make a rather strong statement here:

> **We need to slow way down in our reading
> and pay attention to what the text is saying.
> When we gloss over verses and then assign
> meanings that just sound good, we can end
> up with some very wrong doctrine.**

Now, we come to the fifth verse and the last one I want to look at in this passage (at least at this time). Here we have what very much sounds like the suffering of Jesus surrounding his death. He was pierced, crushed, and punished. This was for our transgressions and iniquities. What this did was bring us two things: peace and healing. Now, here is where we can get into real trouble. We went through this passage and saw what God was trying to say, through Isaiah. We connected certain parts to Matthew, to ensure that the way we were viewing it was correct, but if now, we take verse five and drive its meaning backward to define all the text before it, we end up with some big problems. This is one of the bad practices that has confused this text for over a century in America. So, let's not reinterpret all the text before this verse. Instead, let's take it the same we would any other literature. This is a follow-on idea that is added to what was presented. It does not talk about the same event.

1. This is a continuation of the last part of the fourth verse. This is still part of the "yet" situation. Jesus was a good and righteous man, and yet …

2. Notice the first part of this fifth verse. He was pierced and crushed for what? Our wrongdoing – our sins, right? And, by this punishing act, we are healed.

So, does this means we are well and without any sickness – or if we have enough faith, we will always be well, and always be healed of any illness we have? Hmm. No, no, no! This is not what this passage says. To make this work we have to connect participles that are not supposed to be connected – and we would not do this in any other literature. Here is the kicker: What is Jesus being punished for? Why did he endure those stripes from the whippings? For our sins, not for our disease. Nowhere in this passage does it say that Jesus died for our diseases. It says he died for our sins. So in context, then, what are we being healed from? Disease? No. We are being healed from our sins. In a real and deeply meaningful way, God's plan for the cross was to pay for all sin, for all time, so we could spend eternity with him. The price of that was horrific. It was immeasurable. The price for all that sin was so high that it doesn't even come close to the cost of diseased bodies. We need to remember that this body we have is temporary. Jesus even told his disciples that this flesh accounts for nothing. Jesus healed out of compassion and grace. At the same time, he knew that everybody he healed would succumb to other diseases and eventually to death. Would the Son of God endure the cross for a momentary solution to disease, when he could provide pain and disease-free life for eternity? No. This idea of Jesus dying on the cross to guarantee physical healing for all defies scripture and it defies even common sense.

Conclusions

I have probably drawn more conclusions than I had intended, so you need to be the final judge of what I am presenting. Look at the texts yourself and see what you think. I think, all in all, there are some overarching ideas we can glean from all this.

When we read the Gospels, as well as any other book in the Bible, we need to be very careful how we read it. We should try not to skip over things - even difficult things - unless they are presented as a riddle. We do not need to spend a lot of time figuring out the riddles. They are or will be, more plain sometimes, and at other times the riddles will be beyond our understanding. Learn to let those go. But, for non-riddled text, look at each phrase, as well as the whole passage. Dissect the actual language the way you would any other literature. Read other translations and look up some of the more problematic words in Greek or Hebrew. Be sure you know what the verse says before you move on. Try not to assume. And, what I mean by this is, if there are any oddities, then look them up. If they sound plain and clear, usually digging deeper does not bring any better meaning. In the case of our sample text in Matthew 8, the quote from another verse that is buried in a riddle-style prophecy can be problematic. When this occurs, we need to take the time to make sure we truly understand what the writers are trying to relay. And relax. Most verses in the Bible (outside of prophecy), do not take a whole lot of research if any at all. Most of them will be pretty plain if we do not interject our own ideas.

Chapter 9

The Followers

One of the most influential contributors to the New Testament writings was a murderer. Saul (later called Paul), thought he was doing God a service by wiping out a new Jewish sect that followed the Rabbi, Jesus. Because Jesus had gone back to his Father in heaven, he supernaturally appeared to Paul, and Paul fell to the ground. He recognized that Jesus was the son of God and the Messiah, so he spent the rest of his life serving Jesus and teaching others to follow him. It may seem odd that God would use a murderer for his work, but this is what God does, through Jesus. He changes hearts. He changes people as nobody else can.

The Little Guy

There once was a guy who had a very unreliable car. It would often just stop and refuse to be restarted. He had taken it to several repair shops, but none of them could figure out why it was so temperamental. One day, this guy's car quit as he was going up a slight incline, so as usual he got out and tried pushing the car to a safe place. Since the road went slightly uphill, the man struggled to get it to even move. A passerby saw him struggling, so he stopped to help him. He was a rather large and strong fellow and when the car owner saw him, he was overjoyed. In his mind, this was a heaven-sent answer to his problems. The big guy came over to the car, placed his hands on its back, and shoved with all his might. The car owner also began pushing with renewed energy and the car began to move. They pushed it a little way, but it took all their strength to get it going against that little hill. After about 10 minutes, another guy came along and saw how they were struggling, so he stopped to join in the effort. Now, this guy was only about five feet tall and weighed about 110 pounds. It looked like he didn't have a muscle on his skinny body. The car owner looked and him and just shook his head. He just knew that this was not going to be the help he needed. Immediately the skinny guy went to work on moving that car, so the others quickly joined the effort. To their surprise, the car started moving much more easily and they were able to push it down the road to a safe place. The car owner thanked both of the guys and gave them a very large smile.

So, what is the moral of this story? Well, it may be something like this: Sometimes we may not realize exactly what we need. God has used some very unlikely people to do his will. He knew there was something in specific people that with his help, they could do what they never thought was possible. Jesus' disciples could fit this description. Some were just fishermen, and one was even a tax collector. I think if we consider this, we can start to believe that we can be used by God, also.

More on Paul

After Paul's conversion to Christianity, or what was also called "The Way," in the early church, Paul began to preach and teach about Jesus. Being a very learned Jew, he knew the Old Testament thoroughly. He effectively debated with the Jews, showing them in scripture that Old Testament prophecies matched what Jesus had accomplished. So, instead of killing Christians, he embraced them and spent his life planting new churches, as well as overseeing these churches. One part of this "presbytery", was writing letters to the churches. These letters generally included encouragement and correction, as well as answers to doctrine and issues within the specific church body. The big question today is this: Are letters written to a specific church in the first century, relevant to the twenty-first-century church? Hmm. Well, you may have to answer that one for yourself, as you read the Bible and see if there are any problems today that are similar to the ones the early church encountered.

Get the Shovel

Since this book is about study methods, let's dig into sample texts of Paul's writing.

> **Galatians 3: - 10 For all who rely on the works of the law are under a curse, as it is written: "Cursed is everyone who does not continue to do everything written in the Book**

**of the Law." 11 Clearly no one who relies on
the law is justified before God, because "the
righteous will live by faith." 12 The law is not
based on faith; on the contrary, it says, "The
person who does these things will live by
them." 13 Christ redeemed us from the curse
of the law by becoming a curse for us, for it is
written: "Cursed is everyone who is hung on
a pole." 14 He redeemed us so that the
blessing given to Abraham might come to the
Gentiles through Christ Jesus, so that by
faith we might receive the promise of the
Spirit.**

Go ahead now and make sure you do a Fresh Read of this text.
There are many common Christian principles here, so it will be
hard to separate your thoughts from all the teaching you have
received – but try. Now, what do you see in this text? I see an
argument for faith in place of works (under the Law).
However, we need to be very careful about how we read this
text. We can easily start to believe that everyone who observes
the Law (or whoever did) was under a curse. Many ministers
have preached that this is true, but is this what the text says?
No. It says those who "rely" on his own works. The
referenced text that follows (from the OT) also gives us a clue.

**Deuteronomy 27:26 "Cursed is anyone who
does not uphold the words of this law by
carrying them out."**

When we do our job and look up the actual referenced text, we
see the idea even more clearly. It is not the people who are

under the Law that are cursed, it is the people who do not keep the Law that are cursed. We also know that no one can keep the Law, flawlessly, so perhaps it is this failure by everyone in the OT that brings the curse, and not the Law itself. One thing is for sure: We know that Jesus met a very strong influence to follow the Pharisees, and unfortunately, this cultural and religious influence affected some of the Christian churches. At times there was a very strong push to be like the Pharisees and observe the Law, while at the same time, trying to embrace Christ. It was not working.

Paul goes on to say that anyone who relies on the Law, or in context, those who rely on their ability to observe all of the Law, are not justified in God's eyes. Instead, Paul makes a case for faith being the way to true justification. Paul also seems to say that when Jesus hung on the cross (which was a "tree" or "pole"), he was cursed (under the terms of the Law), so the curse of not being able to keep the Law, fell on him, rather than us.

Paul also, says something that probably enraged the Jews. He said that Jesus redeemed us so "the blessing given to Abraham" could come to the Gentiles also.

So, what do you think this all means? Is this whole passage clear? One thing I see is that there are four scriptures referenced in this short passage of scripture:

- Galatians 3:10 > Deut. 27:26
- Galatians 3:11 > Hab. 2:4
- Galatians 3:12 > Lev. 18:5
- Galatians 3:13 > Deut. 21:23

If you are studying thoroughly, you will look up each of these scriptures and also read the text that surrounds them. I will not do that here, since space and the flow of this book are best served by abstaining.

As you read through our text in Galatians, did you see anything that sounded odd or is not clear? What I am mostly concerned about is terminology. To read this in English and truly understand just what is written on the page, we would need some Bible background. It may not be completely clear what these terms are: the Law; justified; righteous; faith; redeemed. Now, to most readers of this book, at least some of these terms are pretty well known, but if there are some of these that you do not know, please take the time to look them up. You should only have to do this once or twice, and then you will forever know what the Bible is talking about when you see these words. In contrast, if you skip over unfamiliar words, you could be reading in the dark for a long time. Be faithful in your study. You can keep it simple, but you do want to understand the basics of Bible terms.

Though this letter to the Galatian church may have had some difficult ideas for the church to absorb, these should not be too difficult today. Keeping the Law does not make us look right to God. It does not purify us. Only Christ's sacrifice can truly make us presentable to God – pure and blameless. There is a lesson here that Paul was trying to get across to us as Christians, and many churches in the twentieth and twenty-first centuries missed the full meaning of what Paul said. Many churches in the last century have taught or suggested that doing the following things help Christians be more holy:

- Worshipping on Saturday

- Not eating pork

- Circumcision

- Tithing

So, what do you think? Do any of these make us justified before God? Do we get "points" in heaven for doing any of these things? Perhaps some readers are stuck on the last one. After all, it seems every church preaches a strong tithing message, right? Is it not robbery when we do not tithe (from Malachi 3:8)? No, no, no. The directives for tithing were part of the Law and it does not apply to the church. And, the prophecy in Malachi was a directive to the children of Israel and it was for them to obey the Law. Thus, Malachi does not apply to us, either. Furthermore, if we did want to obey the Law on tithing, we would have to do it much differently than we do. The tithing taught in our churches today does not even resemble what the Law required. In short, the tithe was to be brought once a year and your whole extended family was to come (including servants) to the temple and eat it there. What was left remained at the temple, but first there was rather grand feasting on what you had produced, at the temple in the sight of God. Try implementing that in the local church! Oh, and it gets better. Every third year, instead of taking ten percent of your crops to the temple, you would take them to a local storehouse (or if you lived close to the temple, there was a storehouse there). That year, you did not eat any of it. What was in the storehouse was for the poor and needy (such as widows) in your community. Now, try preaching that in the church! Oh, no, we need that money for the utilities or replacing the carpet, or whatever. Though this is very true, it does not follow the Law. So, I must say, either get on board and do it the way the Law says or stop preaching a tradition called "tithing" that is nowhere near what tithing is. The last point is that there is no instruction by any of the Apostles for the church to tithe. However, there is a consistent encouragement to support the local body and churches that need special help. One important difference between the demanded tithe and New Testament giving is that this new giving is to be from a glad heart and not from a feeling of guilt or compulsion. If you would like to see the full picture about tithing, see my book, CHRISTIANS DON'T BE SO GULLIBLE.

Okay, let's go pick on someone else.

Peter

Peter seems to write with straightforward ideas, but readers still need to know basic Bible terms. Let's look at the first chapter of Peter's first letter.

> **1 Peter 1: - 22 Now that you have purified yourselves by obeying the truth so that you have sincere love for each other, love one another deeply, from the heart. 23 For you have been born again, not of perishable seed, but of imperishable, through the living and enduring word of God.**

Read it and see what you get from the text. Is there any weird stuff? Any questions pop into your head? Hmm. I am having a problem right off. What is this phrase, "purified yourself?" I thought only Christ could purify us. Do I need to change my doctrine here? Is Peter saying I can get right with God, through my works? Hmm. I think there is trouble in River City, folks. So, what do we do? Should we pull down five commentaries from the shelf or dive into a collection of related verses? Do word searches? Hmm. Why don't we just relax? If someone quoted these verses to you, or you got these in some literature, or possibly as a social media meme, the first thing you need to do is very simple: Read the rest of the text that surrounds these two verses. Look for the core idea the writer is talking about, then come into these verses with the same mindset as the writer – in this case, the Apostle Peter. Let me help you. This is the text right before these two verses:

> **1 Peter 1: - 17 Since you call on a Father who judges each person's work impartially, live out your time as foreigners here in reverent fear. 18 For you know that it was not with perishable things such as silver or gold that you were redeemed from the empty way of life handed down to you from your ancestors, 19 but with the precious blood of Christ, a lamb without blemish or defect. 20 He was chosen before the creation of the world, but was revealed in these last times for your sake. 21 Through him you believe in God, who raised him from the dead and glorified him, and so your faith and hope are in God.**

> **22 Now that you have purified yourselves by obeying the truth so that you have sincere**

love for each other, love one another deeply, from the heart. 23 For you have been born again, not of perishable seed, but of imperishable, through the living and enduring word of God.

Do you see the context, now? Yeah! Peter says to the Christians he is writing to, that they were redeemed not by perishable valuables, but by the precious blood of Christ. In other words, they did not get right on their own, they were in debt and they had to be redeemed. Christ gave his blood to buy them back. So, then, what is the context of the phrase, "you have purified yourself"? Well, you need to draw your own conclusions, but it seems that Peter is praising them for making the right choice. Instead of trying to be made right by their works, they chose God's plan of redemption through Christ. They said I see that the only way I am going to look right to God is if Christ's blood pays for my sin. That choice of coming to Christ for salvation (instead of observing the Law), allowed them to be purified from their sin. So, as the 22nd verse says, "Now that you have purified yourselves by obeying the truth …" The key phrase is "obeying the truth." When they chose to obey the truth of Jesus' redemption offer, they were purified, as a result of that choice. At least this is what I get from the text.

Do you see any other anomalies in this passage? Any odd terms or phrases? I do not. However, I am wondering about this connection Peter is making between being purified through Christ and having a sincere love for fellow Christians. I see a lot of division and even contempt in the body of Christ today. What is up with that? Maybe we all need to read this more often. See what you think, but it seems that Peter is pointing toward how we were saved and saying "look at that." He seems to be stressing that when we realize how we have been saved, it should produce a genuine love for each other. This is not a "love everybody" doctrine - it is loving your brother and sister in Christ. Still, there seems to be an element of choice here, too. Peter directs the Christians to love each other deeply, from the heart. This is not a showy smile and hugs on Sunday morning.   This is deep respect and admiration for fellow Christians.

Lastly, it seems Peter is telling the church they are "born again." Now, where does this phrase come from? I think if I was a new Christian, and this was one of the first texts I read, I might be a little confused as to what being born again, means. For those of us who have been in the church world for a while, we have an idea of what Peter is talking about. However, as Bible students, we need to practice good study techniques and establish sound doctrine. So, where did this phrase originate? When was it first used and who said it? Let's look.

John 3: - Now there was a Pharisee, a man named Nicodemus who was a member of the Jewish ruling council. 2 He came to Jesus at night and said, "Rabbi, we know that you are a teacher who has come from God. For no one could perform the signs you are doing if God were not with him." 3 Jesus replied, "Very truly I tell you, no one can see the kingdom of God unless they are born again."

This is the first time "born again" is used, at least that I can find in a digital search of the Bible. Are you using RID principles here? I hope so. The text simply says that Nicodemus went to Jesus, secretly, to ask him questions. It sounds like he was open to Jesus' teaching. We might say he was an honest inquirer. Jesus told him that no one could see the kingdom of God unless they were born again. Now, I am not sure how you interpret the word "see," but to me, it would be seeing it firsthand – as in being there inside of it. This could be the same as this verse in the book of Peter.

> **1 Peter 3:10 For, "Whoever would love life and see good days must keep their tongue from evil and their lips from deceitful speech."**

In this verse, the matter of "seeing" is based on what you do first. This is the same kind of caveat Jesus used when he was talking to Nicodemus.

> **If you are going to get that, you must first do this.**

In both of these caveats, there is a "see." I think it is obvious in 1 Peter that the "see" includes participation. It is a first-hand view. You have to be there to "see" the good days. Similarly, in John chapter 3, if Nicodemus wants to get a first-hand view of the kingdom of God, he will need to be standing in it. To see it, he will need to be a member. So, for him to "see" it, he has to be born again. No impure thing enters this kingdom, right? Now, what I presented is only one way of looking at these verses. You will need to apply RID rules to these verses and see what you determine. As much as possible, try to make

God's Word define itself before you go to any outside source. Word and phrase searches or cross-references are the best tools to keep things within the pages of the Bible.

Chapter 10

A Work of Weeding

Everyone just loves weeding, right? Yuk. I detest it, but if things are going to look nice and we want our good plants to survive, weeding is necessary. In Bible study, we also need to be constantly weeding. This is not so much the weeding out of the bad people from the good, it is the weeding out of assumed and created doctrines that do not properly match with the straightforward text that is on the pages of the Bible.

For this section of the book, I want to discuss the prophetic things Jesus said and try to divide between what Jesus did say and what he did not. I want to throw out all of the "filled-in" ideas that have been presented over many years and just look at what Christ said.

Sources of Information

In pursuit of truth, it is always a good idea to look at the person who is providing the truth. Certainly, the son of God was blameless and he got all his doctrine from God his Father, so, we can trust all that he said - but what about other teachers throughout history? Let's look at a couple of authors that have greatly influenced many churches and their doctrines.

Darby

Perhaps one of the most influential figures for questionable church doctrine is John Nelson Darby. He was born in Westminster, London in 1801 and helped form the Plymouth Brethren church/organization. His background is interesting, but it seems that during a time when he was breaking away from the Anglican church and after a nasty fall off of a horse (in 1827), he began writing what could be described as theories about the meaning of certain scripture passages. What emerged, in part, was a million-dollar word that few of the young Sunday morning church attendees have heard: Dispensationalism.

Dispensationalism

Yes, it's a big word and it has had a huge effect on our modern church world. What does it mean? Here is my shortened definition: The theory or doctrine says that God dispenses his grace in measures. Pointing to important events in Biblical history, this doctrine claims that they prove God pours out his grace with special favor at the times of his choosing and then pulls it back until another time of his choosing. Now, to be honest, I've always thought this a bit strange, because it seems to me that the Bible tells us that God's love never fades or diminishes. If his grace is driven by his love (and it is), then how can his grace diminish? How can it be poured out at one time in history and then pulled back at other times? You can believe what you wish and you very well may be right, but I would like to offer another possible explanation: Perhaps God's chosen actions have nothing to do with the strength of his grace. Perhaps his historical timing is just that; crucial and strategic timing that capitalizes on cultures and events to maximize impact. Perhaps God is working very actively, every day, as he always has, for all men and making his grace known to all who seek him.

Along with the establishment of Dispensationalism, there was also Pre-Millennialism and an upsurge in Futurism. Wow, more fancy words. To make it short, this simply means Darby taught that Christians were going to be taken away, or "raptured," before a 7 year tribulation period. His base of futurism beliefs claimed that the book of Revelation was all or mostly about events that were to happen at a future date (after the early 1800s). What is odd about what he taught, is that no other Christian church taught or believed those things. In fact, it seems that no Christian church in history ever believed the doctrine he started teaching. So, guess what happened? He was branded as a heretic and his teaching was rejected by the Christian church. However, he didn't stop teaching it and trying to gain followers. The era when this new doctrine was launched was in the 1830s and it stayed fairly small in impact until 1909. So, it seems that for over seventy years, Darby's doctrines were not widely accepted and they might have even been in danger of falling into obscurity. However, in 1909 a remarkable thing happened. A respected Theologian by the name of Cyrus Ingerson Scofield published his study bible that included much of Darby's doctrines. Of course, what happens when people have a Bible where on the same page as scripture, there is an explanation of the passage? It makes those notes much more believable and in some ways, for some people, it makes the explanations nearly as authoritative as the Bible text. One seldom talked about aspect of this whole scenario is that at least at one point in Scofield's life, he did some very questionable (criminal) things and associated with dishonest people. As a leader in the church world, divorce was not at all accepted during his life, and yet, it seems he left his wife and children, and later married another woman. There is also a question about him adopting the title of a doctor when it appears he did not complete any approved courses that would grant him the title. Now, there may be other answers to why all these things seem to have occurred and are written in books about him, but the question remains as to his true character. He also seemed to be heavily influenced by "Zionist," who certainly were not Christian.

Here is my central point about these Biblical teachers: I encourage you to check the lives and teachings of both Darby and Scofield before you summarily accept their Biblical views.

<u>The Impact</u>

It wasn't long after Darby's doctrines were popularized by Scofield's Study Bible, that Christian churches started teaching this new and exciting doctrine. Slowly, but surely, the doctrine that was once hailed as heresy, became the main-stream theories of tribulation, rapture, and the millennial reign of Christ. In more recent times, a flood of books, movies, and training materials have been produced that support Darby's unique doctrine.

So, what are we to do with this Dispensationalism when we look at Revelation? Well, the bottom line is that we shelf it during the study, until after we have looked at everything objectively. Does this mean you can't or shouldn't believe Darby's claims? No, this is not what I am saying. Even if some prophecies have already occurred somewhere in history, these prophecies could occur again. There are other instances in God's Word, where prophecies were fulfilled and yet they were also to be fulfilled again at a later time. The real issue we have in making sure things are placed on the Altar of Truth is that whatever we believe is well-proven in scripture. If we have to manipulate and twist things to make them fit what we believe to be true, then we have violated a most sacred responsibility to seek the truth.

To Weed

To weed out questionable doctrines and ideas, as I said, we need to look closely at the source of ideas. If the authors of certain doctrines or ways of viewing God's Word, have questionable expertise or seem to be teaching very unique things, we need to investigate the validity of what they teach. And, once we have become mature in Christ, we are duty-bound to test and prove every doctrine we hear. When we find ourselves mesmerized or hanging on every word a Bible teacher says, and drinking it all in, with no filters or checklists in place, we can easily get caught up in false doctrines. Why? Because false doctrines are usually tailored toward making people feel good – or terrorizing them mercilessly. These are means of control. In some ways, false doctrines are a little like a Ponzi scheme. The teachers keep stringing you along with glossy-sounding promises. As soon as you get close to one of the limits to their claims, then they alter their story to get you to continue. Whether this is a claim of horrible disaster, the end of the world, or Jesus' second (or third) coming, the idea is the same. What is odd, is when it pretty much all breaks down, many continue to blindly follow. If I can use Darby as an example, he taught that Jesus' return was imminent and insisted on a very soon return. That was nearly 200 years ago. That is not what I would call imminent. Scofield claimed the same thing, about 70 years later. What is quite interesting, is that in another corner of America, Joseph Smith, who was the founder of the Church of Jesus Christ of Latter-Day Saints (LDS, Mormons), seemed to be saying similar things. He lived from 1805 to 1844, so he was in the same period as Darby, yet what Joseph Smith was teaching was heresy. It was not at all Christian. Now, you will need to check the following information yourself to decide whether you believe it or not, because some in the Mormon Church claim this is not true, yet their documents say differently. Here is what I found in my research:

It seems that Joseph Smith called a meeting of his church leaders in February 1835 to tell them that he had spoken to God and learned that Jesus would return within the next 56 years, after which the End Times would begin promptly. The result of this revelation is documented in the "Doctrine and Covenants" at 130:14-17 (by Joseph Smith). Here is an excerpt from that document:

14 I was once praying very earnestly to know the time of the coming of the Son of Man, when I heard a voice repeat the following: 15

"Joseph, my son, if thou livest until thou art eighty-five years old, thou shalt see the face of the Son of Man; therefore let this suffice, and trouble me no more on this matter." 16 I was left thus, without being able to decide whether this coming referred to the beginning of the millennium or to some previous appearing, or whether I should die and thus see his face. 17 I believe the coming of the Son of Man will not be any sooner than that time.

Oddly, we see a similar theme in the Mormon movement as with what Darby was teaching. So, if one very false cult is teaching the same things as Christianity, shouldn't this raise some red flags? And, if claim after claim of Christ's return in a few years or within a person's lifetime, fails over and over, shouldn't this raise more flags? If prophets in the Christian church arise and say that Jesus will return within a certain person's life, and it does not happen, wouldn't that prophet be considered to be a false prophet? Doesn't the Biblical standard to test the validity of a prophet pivot on whether what he foretells comes true? If it does not, isn't he considered to be a fraud?

Here is a little personal tidbit. In a church I attended when I was about 25 years old, there was an older pastor who believed that God gives special Spiritual gifts. I also believed that and still do. It seems to be proven by several Biblical texts. One of these gifts is a gift of prophecy. Now, this gift is not known in all churches, so I think I need to say that prophecies by people who are given this gift, can be for a group or one person.

When they are for one person, it is often called "personal prophecy." This reference keeps people from thinking that what was said to one person was for all. Here is the application of that gifting regarding this older pastor. I was in his office one day, and he said that a person who was supposed to have this prophetic gift, told the pastor he would not die before Jesus would return (that is, he would be raptured). The pastor firmly believed this and told everyone, proudly. Sadly, he passed away many years ago. The prophecy was false, and though this man was a good and honest minister, he firmly believed he would be raptured before we died, and he was not.

Testing and proving everything is important, and this includes our beliefs about the future. So, to weed out ideas that are more fantasy than fact, we need to look at things that Jesus and his followers taught about their future. Now, some readers might think there was a typo in the last sentence, but there was not. I did say "their, "future, not "our" future. Everything that Jesus said about the future was said, directly to the disciples and it was for their benefit. Unlike commandments in the Old Testament and the Law, there is no indication in the four Gospel books that Jesus told his disciples to write down the things he told them about the future and pass them on to future generations. He gave them specific directions that called for them to take action. At least that is the way I take his words. When you read them, see what you think, but again, only consider what is written, not what is filled in or manipulated.

Dig it

Now, that I have laid out some ways we can eliminate things that impair a Fresh Read, let's look at some things Jesus said.

First, I want to look at a prophetic parable.

> **Matthew 13:36-43 --- Then he left the crowd and went into the house. His disciples came to him and said, "Explain to us the parable of the weeds in the field." He answered, "The one who sowed the good seed is the Son of Man. The field is the world, and the good seed stands for the people of the kingdom. The weeds are the people of the evil one, and the enemy who sows them is the devil. The harvest is the end of the age, and the harvesters are angels. "As the weeds are pulled up and burned in the fire, so it will be at the end of the age. The Son of Man will send out his angels, and they will weed out of his kingdom everything that causes sin and all who do evil. They will throw them into the blazing furnace, where there will be weeping and gnashing of teeth. Then the righteous will shine like the sun in the kingdom of their Father. Whoever has ears, let them hear.**

Okay, since we are partnering in this study of Jesus' prophetic words, what did you get from Jesus' explanation? In all honesty, if you have heard many sermons and/or been in Bible studies for very long, you will have heard a lot of teaching on this parable. I think the basic explanation is pretty clear. Jesus is planting the good seed, which is the Good News of God's salvation. Others in the world who are working for the "Evil One," are planting bad /evil messages that thwart the spreading of the Good News. Notice that Jesus says, "The field is the world, and the good seed stands for the people of the kingdom." Since Jesus is talking about people who are living at that time (or it includes them), the "people of the kingdom" seem to be the believers who have grown up as a result of the seeds Jesus planted. They become "seeds" themselves. So, here is yet another possible clue about the kingdom of heaven or the kingdom of God that John and Jesus were preaching about. Of course, this calls for some deduction, so I will leave you to interpret it as you see fit.

Now, since we are taking a fresh look at Jesus' prophetic teachings, we must consider the future aspect of what Jesus taught. In fact, we are only looking at this parable because it contains statements about the future of the people Jesus was talking to. So, let's take a close look at this portion of the parable:

> **"The harvest is the end of the age, and the**
> **harvesters are angels. "As the weeds are**
> **pulled up and burned in the fire, so it will be**
> **at the end of the age. The Son of Man will**
> **send out his angels, and they will weed out of**
> **his kingdom everything that causes sin and**
> **all who do evil. They will throw them into**
> **the blazing furnace, where there will be**
> **weeping and gnashing of teeth. Then the**
> **righteous will shine like the sun in the**
> **kingdom of their Father."**

What I see here is a foretelling of an event (or possibly more than one), where God's angels "harvest" the weeds (bad seed), and then the wheat (good seed). Those who insisted on spreading malicious messages that led others astray were "burned up." This could be physical or spiritual (soul), but since in Christianity it is commonly believed that a soul lives forever and does not die, this seems it would be more likely physical destruction since it is "burned up" instead of in "pain or agony." Again, after your research, you can make your own conclusions. Just be careful here to not read things into the text. Take it for what it says and nothing more.

Now, moving on to the remainder of this parable's explanation, it seems to me Jesus is saying that after the bad seed is destroyed, then the good seed can shine, and not be overshadowed or thwarted by the bad seed. One thing I did notice about this parable is there seems to be no specific talk about anyone going to heaven or hell. The good seed does not seem to be taken anywhere. Using just the text alone, it seems to me that it is saying the good seed will shine, where they are. The wheat is gathered, but left where it is, whereas the bad seed is gathered and burned up. Now, highly controversial questions here can be phrased something like this: Were those people who spread bad seeds punished with fire on this earth? Was this during Jesus' time or after? Were those who represent the good seed gathered together and protected to live on? If any historical events might satisfy this parable, is it possible Jesus was referring to those future events, versus a soul judgment after this life? Could it be both? Hmm. Study, study, my friend. The answers are likely there within the pages of your Bible.

Let's move on and take a look at a critical yet simple concept in Jesus' prophecies.

What is The End?

There are things Jesus said that seem to be time-sensitive, and these things often trip-up Bible scholars who are trying to make sense of Eschatology. Let's look first at two verses in Matthew.

> **Matthew 10:23 - "But whenever they persecute you in one city, flee to the next; for truly I say to you, you will not finish going through the cities of Israel until the Son of Man comes."**

> **Matthew 24:14 - "This gospel of the kingdom shall be preached in the whole world as a testimony to all the nations, and then the end will come."**

Before we jump into these, I think it is important to point out that in Eschatology, these verses are sometimes seen as separate prophecies, thus, they are not required to be the same idea or time frame. In all fairness, if we read the book of Matthew in the way we read any other literature, we do see these verses separately. Since one is in the tenth chapter, we might not even remember it by the time we got to the twenty-fourth chapter. So, when we talk about these verses you are perfectly right to separate the ideas. However, for this book, I want to talk about the subject matter of these verses. Listing them together is just more for convenience than eschatological accuracy.

Now, as you read these verses (separately or together), how would you interpret them, if this was the first time you saw them? Is there anything odd about them? Are there words or phrases that seem odd?   I don't see strange symbolism or odd phrasing, so I think I can skip the "I" in our RID rules. The first thing I see in Matthew 10:23 is that Jesus is telling the disciples they are going to be persecuted. I am going to stop myself right here and contemplate this. Historically, were the disciples persecuted after Jesus ascended? Yes, absolutely. So we know what Jesus said came true and we know the time frame of when it happened.

The next part of Matthew 10:23 is tricky to some scholars but does not need to be. Let's just see what it says without any fancy footwork.

> **"… you will not finish going through the cities of Israel until the Son of Man comes."**

Big mystery here, right? I mean all the Eschatology experts really need to fight over the meaning of this short passage, right? Hmm. Well, I am not sure what you get from this text, but it seems pretty clear to me. Jesus seems to be saying that the disciples are going to obey his command to go out and spread the Good News through all the cities of Israel, and yet, they will not complete the task before Jesus returns. What? Wait. Does this sound like Jesus is going to delay thousands of years? No. But, even if I have doubts about how this could be true, I have to admit that the text itself seems to be pretty clear. I guess the big question we have here is more mathematical. Can we calculate how much time it would take for 12 or more people to preach the Good News to all of the major cities of Israel? Even on foot, maybe it would take just a few years. I did notice one thing here that Jesus did not say. He didn't say that the Good News would necessarily be heard by every living soul by the time he returned. Jesus only says that the disciples would go through the cities of Israel, preaching the Good News.

I want to emphasize this again, as I did in my other book: Whether we are comfortable or not with what we read in the Bible, we need to protect its integrity by not changing what it says. If this twenty-third verse says that the disciples would not completely evangelize Israel before he returned, then that is what Jesus meant. He would not lie. Exactly how he accomplished this may be a mystery to many scholars, but we cannot escape a difficult piece of the Bible by changing what it says to meet our predetermined doctrine. Either Jesus said this and meant it, or he didn't. The worst thing we can do is violate the "D" in our RID rules and play God. If we act like we are God and overrule what is written in his Word, we become irresponsible in protecting one of the most sacred things on this planet. Again, we must read what is on the page and interpret it without manipulation.

Now, let's look at the other verse.

> **Matthew 24:14 - "This gospel of the kingdom shall be preached in the whole world as a testimony to all the nations, and then the end will come."**

First things, first: Does this verse say the same as the previous verse? I am going to say, no. The verse in chapter 10, talks about preaching the Good News to the cities of Israel, and this verse talks about preaching to the whole world. Now, I have a real problem here. The same writer has recorded that Jesus said the disciples would not finish preaching to all Israel before his return, yet here Matthew records Jesus as saying that the Good News will be preached in the "whole world" before the "end" comes. What do you think about this? Let me share this thought: Since I said we could use mathematics to calculate how long it would take to evangelize Israel, let's do some math for how long it takes to evangelize the world. Wow. It sounds daunting, doesn't it? But, one thing we can do is combine tasks. What if Israel was being preached to at the same time as the rest of the world? The math results would be slightly different. Now, let's consider something else. Let's keep this whole situation in context. Jesus is talking to the disciples about the "world." Jesus knew how they received what he said, right? Yes, he did. So, when the disciples and their friends talked about "the world," did they think about America? Absolutely not. They did not know about America (north or south). Generally speaking, the regions outside the known civilized world were not considered (at that time and in that culture), to be part of "the world." So, if Jesus was meaning the "known civilized world," the task would be reasonable to what Jesus' followers could do. They started with about 120 believers, according to the first chapter of Acts, and then by the end of Chapter 2, there were 3000 more. Persecution came later and it forced the Christians to leave Jerusalem and even Judea. So, they spread out and carried the Good News to extended regions. Also, it is a historical fact that the Apostle Thomas followed the oriental trade routes down into the China region. He planted churches all along that route and many are still there (or at least the evidence of their existence). In fact, with the work of Paul, and so many other missionary workers, the Good News was spread to all the major regions of the known civilized world within the first century. It took a lot of people, but with each conversion, the task became easier. So, without manipulating Matthew 24:14, is it possible that both of these tasks, Israel and the world, could have been fulfilled by the time Jesus said he would return? It is an interesting question and not easy to answer, regardless of your end-time view. Even if we can rightfully say that this is possible, we have an even larger issue to address. What does "the end" mean? Is this the same event as Jesus' return? It could be and in fact, there are some suggestions in scripture that the disciples believed so. But does the text in either of these verses or the parables we looked at, demand that "the end" is the same event as Jesus' return? Hmm. I would say no. It is possible, but not demanded.

Because there is much controversy over what "the end" means in any scripture, let's take a closer look at this – but let's first look at this verse again.

> **Matthew 24:14 - "This gospel of the kingdom shall be preached in the whole world as a testimony to all the nations, and then the end will come."**

If we focus on the phrase, "the end will come," I am going to assume the "will" means that it will wait until the preaching is completed (or God says, okay you got it covered). When you look at this you may see it differently, of course.

Time to engage the "I" in RID. "The end" is an odd phrase. Not because the words are unfamiliar in our current terms, but because it is not well defined in these verses. When common phrases are not defined like this, it can be because the speaker knows his listeners understand the terms he is using. So, we will need to look elsewhere in the Bible to see what Jesus is talking about. We may even find other verses in Matthew that define this phrase. I suggest you do a digital search of the Bible and see where "the end" occurs. There may be many, so you may need to weed out the ones that do not apply to end times.

Here is a little tidbit you might find interesting: As I am writing this book, I am also doing research. So, I stopped my writing between the last paragraph and this one to do a digital search of the Bible (NIV) for the phrase "the end." As I suspected, the search produced a lot of results. In fact, 166 places in the Bible use this phrase. Let me share a few with you. The first is in Genesis 8:33 and it has to do with the flood.

1. Genesis 8:3 "The water receded steadily from the earth. At the end of the hundred and fifty days the water had gone down …"

2. Exodus 23:16 - "At the end of the 430 years, to the very day, all the Lord's divisions left Egypt."

3. 1 Kings 8:10 - At the end of twenty years, during which Solomon built these two buildings—the temple of the Lord and the royal palace –

4. 2 Kings 24:20 - It was because of the Lord's anger that all this happened to Jerusalem and Judah, and in the end he thrust them from his presence.

5. Matthew 13:39-40 --- and the enemy who sows them is the devil. The harvest is the end of the age, and the harvesters are angels.

6. Matthew 13:49 - This is how it will be at the end of the age. The angels will come and separate the wicked from the righteous.

7. Matthew 24:3 (same chapter as the verse we are studying) - As Jesus was sitting on the Mount of Olives, the disciples came to him privately. "Tell us," they said, "when will this happen, and what will be the sign of your coming and of the end of the age?"

Now that we have some results, let's see how we can apply these verses to our subject verse (Matthew 24:14). As a reminder, we are trying to resolve a problem with Matthew 24:14, that came to light when we applied the "I" in our RID rules. The phrase "the end" did not seem to be well defined, at least within the verse itself. The search we did may bring in other concepts and uses of this phrase in God's Word, thus we may get a better definition of the phrase. So, let's jump into this and see what these sample verses show us.

One thing I noticed in this search is that in most cases it seemed our phrase "the end" was used in connection with a time frame. This is important as we look at other uses, so file it away in the back of your head. In other cases, our phrase was used for the end of objects. For instance, the end of a garment's tassel or the ends of the earth. The verse in 2 Kings 24:20 may be an exception to these usual usages, however (see below).

2 Kings 24:20

> **"It was because of the Lord's anger that all**
> **this happened to Jerusalem and Judah, and**
> **in the end he thrust them from his presence."**

At least in the NIV, it seems this is not time oriented. That is, there are no days, months or years stated. This is not something that God said is going to happen in a certain month of the year. It seems to say that "the end" is when God completes what he had planned. This idea is likely another key in deciphering what Jesus meant by "the end." So, let's also file this idea away for later use.

Perhaps one of the most significant verses in our search is in Matthew 13.

Matthew 13:39-40

> **"… and the enemy who sows them is the**
> **devil. The harvest is the end of the age, and**
> **the harvesters are angels."**

Does this sound familiar? It is part of Jesus' explanation of a parable we studied earlier. Remember the story about the good seed (wheat) and the bad seed (weeds)? In the passage listed above, Jesus said that the harvest of both the wheat and the weeds, is "the end" of the age, and he said those who do the harvesting are the angels (not us). This seems like a pretty good definition, but our phrase is connected with another term, "end of the age." And, the verse we are studying, is not connected with this phrase. So, we have another question that might help define our original phrase. When Jesus said, "the end" in Matthew 24:14, was he talking about the same thing as "the end of the age" in Matthew 13? Hmm.

As we explore this idea of "the end" and "the end of the age," we can't ignore the reason why Jesus is talking to his disciples about this subject. If we are doing thorough studies, we need to take all of this in its context. For what we started studying (Good News needing to be preached before Jesus' return), we jumped into verses that were part of a much larger discussion. So, let's go back to the beginning of Matthew 24 and try to see the premise for the later verses. Here is Matthew 24:3

> **As Jesus was sitting on the Mount of Olives, the disciples came to him privately. "Tell us," they said, "when will this happen, and what will be the sign of your coming and of the end of the age?"**

Okay, now I got it. The disciples asked Jesus when the things he told them before would happen and added a question about the "end of the age." Now, you need to draw your own conclusions about all this, but I am going to say that when Jesus said "the end" later, in verse 14, he was likely referring to the disciples' question about "the end of the age."

Now that we have some context and some other uses of this phrase in the Bible, we can more easily see that not everywhere in the Bible is the phrase "the end" used the same way. It is possible that even within the New Testament, we may find this same phrase when studying Eschatology, and yet the usage may be different. "The end" may not always mean the same thing or the same events. On the flip side, it is also possible that regarding prophetic scriptures in the New Testament, this phrase could always mean the same thing. Study and context will be your friend in sorting it all out. Before we leave the study of this phrase, let me give you what I think is the clarifying factor.

One thing we have not yet done is to look at the definition of the Greek word(s) used for "the end." Here is what part of Thayer's Geek Lexicon says:

STRONGS NT 5056: τέλος (telos)

8.   End: a) termination, the limit at which a thing ceases to be, (in the Greek writings always of the end of some act or state, but not of the end of a period of time …)

The Greek word sounds like "telos," and as you can see from the definition, it is the termination of an action or event. It seems that one thing it is not is an end of a time period. So, we can rightfully conclude that when Jesus said "the end," in chapter 24, he was meaning the culmination of actions. I may be assuming too much here, but I am thinking, based on the context, that these were actions done by either the Apostles (church) or by God – or both.

This seems pretty neatly tied up, but what about the disciples' question? Well, when you go to your Greek word expository (or dictionary), - and, yes, you need to be doing this – you will find that when the disciples asked Jesus about the "end of the age," the Greek word is different. It sounds like "synteleia," and it means completion, consummation, or end. This term could include the end of a time period, but seems to me to include a little broader use - so it could likely mean the completion of actions or the completion of a time period. If we take another look at this whole picture, we may see indications that the disciples were wanting defined dates and times or at least days or months. Before Jesus ascended, he did tell the disciples that the dates and times were not going to be told and that he didn't even know. So, again, there are texts that sound like Jesus' disciples were like us. They desperately wanted to know exactly when bad things were going to happen and when Jesus was returning. If they thought anything like me, they probably thought that if they knew the "when," they could better prepare for it. But, they couldn't really prepare in a physical sense for what they would experience, and for what was coming to Judea, anyway. So, knowing probably would have just freaked them out. The bottom line is that Jesus talked in terms of the completion of certain necessary things before his return, rather than the passage of time. This seems completely appropriate for a God who is timeless.

Considering the whole picture we have now (or at least the larger canvas) when we study end-times in the Bible, we can remember that the phrase "the end" may not always be referring to the same thing. I think we can rightfully say,

> **In God's view, the completion of certain things he has planned is more useful as eschatological milestones than dates on the calendar.**

More?

I am pretty sure by now, that you are worn out from looking at the prophetic writings of Jesus, and my intention is not to look at this whole picture here. We have barely scratched the surface of what Jesus said. However, if you are interested in looking at the whole tapestry of what Jesus said about end-times, please get my book, JESUS' WORDS WITHOUT INFLAMMATION. In that book, I show how to use the RID rules to fairly evaluate what Jesus said and what he did not say. For now, I want to show you how to do a Fresh Read in other areas of God's Word.

Chapter 11

The Most Misunderstood Book

If the Book of Revelation was a living organism, it would be so inflamed that it would likely die. Why? Because, it has become so bloated, manipulated, and "Hollywood-ized" that it's nearly impossible to separate the truth from fantasy. Somehow, somewhere, there must be a way to pierce through all this hype and truly see what the author intended – or at least, what he did not intend. I believe there's a way to do just that. Thus, I've dedicated this book to helping people clean out speculation, twisted scripture, and right down bad doctrine, from their Bible study toolboxes. How am I going to do this? By giving you yet another doctrine and declaring that it is the only correct view? Absolutely not. What we're going to do, together, is figure out a simple way to clear out the junk and dissipate the smoke that covers a beautiful encouragement from Jesus Christ. Once we do that, you will have a better chance of seeing Revelation as the author intended. From there, what conclusions you draw are strictly between you and Jesus – with no prophecy mongers to interfere.

The Robot

I heard a story once, about a man who spent hundreds of dollars to get a certified original or replica of a robot that is used in a popular science fiction movie. Of course, he ordered it online, and the only pictures in the ad were of the robot as it was in the movies, not the actual product. Because the cost was high, he was sure the robot would be just fantastic. When the package arrived, he was like a kid at Christmas. He quickly tore open the box and inspected its contents. It didn't take long before he discovered his mistake. The box included mostly plans and some stickers. He was to take the box and cut it into the shape of the robot and put the stickers on the outside. Now, he did follow the instructions and built the robot, but it did not look anything like the robot in the movie. It was more like a toddler's toy.

I think we have all had disappointments with things we have ordered online. I have. What is the lesson we all learned? Well, not all sellers are honest - but also sometimes pictures do not show things as they really are. So, why do we all keep buying things online? I think in many ways, we want to believe that our concept of what will happen is correct. Once we create an idea, we own it. Once we own it, we cannot let go of it. It is sometimes like an obsession. We see this in religion, politics, and even in science. Some ideas are just hard to let go of, even when they are dead wrong. When reading the Bible, this concept becomes critical. If we read scripture, or are taught by someone else, we take in thoughts and form complete ideas. If we get it wrong, it is very hard to let it go and hold on to what is right. If we have been in church for years, we have heard preachers and teachers talk about God's Word - but was teaching always correct? We would like to think so, and yet we know in the core of our being and our experience that no person can be right, all the time. The best and more honest people can make mistakes. When we add this to the fact that even the best Bible scholars do not agree on everything, then we need to take a big step backward and re-evaluate what we have heard. When it comes to Revelation and prophecy in general, we have problems right out of the gate. Why? Well, many people do not know why and yet it is as simple as the nose on our face. Again, I would like to remind you of what God said to Aaron and Miriam:

> **Numbers 12:6-8 --- "… he (God) said, "Listen to my words: "When there is a prophet among you, I, the Lord, reveal myself to them in visions, I speak to them in dreams. 7 But this is not true of my servant Moses; he is faithful in all my house. 8 With him I speak face to face, clearly and not in riddles; he sees the form of the Lord.""**

So, the only way to truly decipher Revelation is to first see what it says and what it does not – then look at what Jesus explained. What is not explained is left as a riddle. It may be clear once the prophecy is fulfilled, but until then, unless God tells us more at a later time, it remains a riddle.

Bull Dozer

Okay, for some books, we need to get a shovel and go to work on the text. For Revelation, we need more like a bulldozer. Well, that is the way it feels sometimes, but let me help make it easier. Let's just take each verse and read what is on the page. You will be surprised how much you can get out of Revelation, if you just read it straight, with no interjected ideas. Much of it is not all that mysterious. Let's take a look at how it begins.

The First Paragraph

I don't plan to copy the entire book of Revelation into this book, but from time to time, I will paste in short excerpts so textual exploration is easier. Here is the first paragraph of the book:

> **"The revelation from Jesus Christ, which
> God gave him to show his servants what must
> soon take place. He made it known by
> sending his angel to his servant John, who
> testifies to everything he saw—that is, the
> word of God and the testimony of Jesus
> Christ. Blessed is the one who reads aloud
> the words of this prophecy, and blessed are
> those who hear it and take to heart what is
> written in it, because the time is near."**

Wait; hold on. Before we jump in, let's apply our RID rules. First, let's just read it and see what it says. Let's pretend we have never seen this before. What does this say? Here's what I get: Something has been revealed that is soon to take place. I guess this suggests it has not been known before - or it is expanded information - or a new view of what was known before.

1. The information came from Jesus. Obviously, not from Jesus when he was walking this earth, but from Jesus in Heaven. And, this information that Jesus had was given to him by his Father, God.

2. The information was made known to John by an angel that was sent by Jesus.

3. John is a witness to the things he saw and is willing to testify about what he saw. So, what did he see? It was described here as the "word of God" and the "testimony of Jesus Christ." Pretty simple to me (though it's stated in a rather profound way): What John saw (and heard) was from God and his son!

4. People who read the prophecy out loud are blessed, and so are those who hear it and take it seriously. My take is that since there were no printing presses if many people were going to hear this prophetic message, then someone would have to read it to groups of people.

5. Finally, the reason they will be blessed, if they take it to heart, is because "the time is near."

If I summarized all this, I might say it this way: God wants to tell a group of people something important that is going to happen soon and if they take it seriously, they will be much better off. Now, I'm not saying I see this all correctly, but do you see what I did there? One thing I didn't do is bring in ideas of, "I supposed this" or "Maybe that." I just read it like I would any other book and in my head, I summarized what I thought the author was trying to say.

Let's apply our other rules. Is there anything weird in this passage? Well, I don't see any dragons, beasts, or unfamiliar creatures. This passage seems to have quite familiar phrases, so we don't need to go searching for parallel scripture or similar images. How about our third rule? Well, it seems pretty clear that there is nothing to explain since there are not any details revealed here. We seem to be told that something is going to take place and that it will be soon, but we have not yet been told what these things are.

One final note about this first paragraph: It sounds like someone wrote it after John's original letter because it reads like an explanation of what the letter contains. Not knowing any outside facts, it could have been written by John, but then my question is this: Why would the text say it was a revelation God gave to "him." Wouldn't it say, the revelation God gave to me? In comparison, we are going to see that in the next paragraph, the text begins like a normal letter and says, "John, to the 7 churches …" This is why we need to just read things plainly and wisely.

A Gracious Greeting

> **Revelation 1:- 4 John, To the seven churches**
> **in the province of Asia: Grace and peace to**
> **you from him who is, and who was, and who**
> **is to come, and from the seven spirits[a]**
> **before his throne, 5 and from Jesus Christ,**
> **who is the faithful witness, the firstborn from**

the dead, and the ruler of the kings of the earth. To him who loves us and has freed us from our sins by his blood, 6 and has made us to be a kingdom and priests to serve his God and Father—to him be glory and power for ever and ever! Amen. 7 "Look, he is coming with the clouds," and "every eye will see him, even those who pierced him"; and all peoples on earth "will mourn because of him." So shall it be! Amen. 8 "I am the Alpha and the Omega," says the Lord God, "who is, and who was, and who is to come, the Almighty."

When I read this section (vs 4), I can easily see that this letter was written to 7 churches in what was called "Asia." When I looked at a Biblical or Ancient map (easily seen on the internet) I can see that this area is now the western region of Turkey. So, as we go through this first part of Revelation, keep in mind where this message is targeted (geographically) and to who it is being written.

One thing I would like to point out before we go much further is how gracious John is when writing this letter. It seems to be the forwarding of a friendly message from God himself. There is a favorable language that talks about the love of Christ, what he has done for us, and praise to him. To me, this is a very good feeling introduction and is the tone that God wanted to set for everything that Jesus showed John and the tone he wanted to pass on to the 7 churches. Though we will hear about some terrifying imagery and some strong words of rebuke to the churches, Christ and John are relaying hope and the overwhelming love that God has for the people in the 7 churches. What John was shown was intended to help the people in these 7 churches and to encourage them; not to bring them fear. I would encourage you, then when you read Revelation, and if you teach about it, that you escape the temptation many other teachers have fallen into; that is to use the imagery in Revelation as a means to make people afraid of future events. Fear can be a tool of manipulation, and if we're not careful, we can be guilty of replacing the work of the Holy Spirit, whose job it is to convict people of sin. As children of God, we should never be coercive with the Gospel. The importance of Christ's sacrifice stands on its own and the work of the Holy Spirit is incredibly powerful. We need to just speak the word and let God do the rest.

Moving on to verse 7, we can quickly see that we need to invoke our second rule of RID. We need to ask ourselves, does this sound weird? If you were reading this for the first time, would you judge this as just normal talk? I mean who says "He is coming in the clouds …"? I don't know your thoughts, but as a first read I have no clue what is being said. So, let's see if we can find somewhere else in scripture where there is talk of coming in clouds. The Bible text seems symbolic; so are these real clouds or do they represent something else, or what? Good questions, right? Maybe you also have some other questions about this, so let's do a simple and easy search of the Bible and see what pops up.

Yureka!

Searching through a digital copy of the NIV version of the Bible, I found some interesting passages: In Deuteronomy 33, Moses pronounces a blessing on Israel, shortly before he dies.

Verse 26 talks about God riding on the heavens and on the clouds and verse 27 talks about driving out the enemy.

> **Deuteronomy 33: 26 "There is no one like the God of Jeshurun (Israel), who rides on the heavens to help you and on the clouds in his majesty. 27 The eternal God is your refuge, and underneath are the everlasting arms. He will drive out your enemy before you, saying, 'Destroy him!'"**

The symbolism in this Old Testament passage is similar to the one in Revelation, but you will need to judge whether this helps define our text. Certainly, there were learned Jews, as well as some Christians who would know this text in Deuteronomy and relate it to what John wrote. However, since this is not necessarily a slam dunk for defining what Jesus is saying to John, let's look at a few more examples:

> **Psalms 68:4 "Sing to God, sing praise to his name, extol him who rides on the clouds"**

> **Jeremiah 4:13 "Look! He advances like the clouds, his chariots come like a whirlwind, his horses are swifter than eagles. Woe to us! We are ruined!"**

> **Daniel 7:13 "In my vision at night I looked, and there before me was one like a son of man, coming with the clouds of heaven. He approached the Ancient of Days and was led into his presence."**

In these Old Testament passages, it seems that God is seen as the one who is above everyone and has much greater power than man. The imagery seems to show high respect for God's position and power, but this is my take on these passages. You will need to dissect them yourself and see what applies. One thing seems pretty clear to me: Both God and the "son of man" (Jesus) come with clouds or ride on clouds. Since this is a very old and well-established image of God and his attributes, it would probably be erroneous to say that our text in Revelation is showing something new about Jesus or is talking about a new event. The referral to Jesus and clouds seems to me to be more about who he is rather than something is going to do. But, that's what I get. You need to make up your mind. Now, before we leave this subject of clouds, let's look at what Jesus said when he was living here on earth:

> **Matthew 24:30 "At that time the sign of the Son of Man will appear in the sky, and all the nations of the earth will mourn. They will see the Son of Man coming on the clouds of the sky, with power and great glory."**

> **Mark 13:26 "At that time men will see the Son of Man coming in clouds with great power and glory."**

To be fair, there are a couple more verses in the Gospel books that echo the verses above, but to save time, these will do. In the two verses above, Jesus is talking about what was referred to as "the end of the age," and the destruction of the temple in Jerusalem. It also refers to Jesus' second coming, but we need to be careful here that we don't jump to conclusions about

Jesus second coming. One thing does seem to be pretty simple here, however: When Jesus appears in clouds, it is with power and glory and that is in contrast to his first coming where he was God's humble servant and a lamb to be slain.

Seals?

Early in the fifth chapter of Revelation, Jesus starts showing John what has likely been sealed up for a long time. No one else, not even the angels in heaven, had been shown what John is about to see. So what is it that Jesus is going to reveal? The very first verse of this chapter, says that God (the one on the throne), has a scroll in his hand and it has writing on both sides. To me, this says that what this document contains is not a short message. Of course, you should draw your own conclusions. After John notices the scroll, we have a new player in this heavenly scene: It's a mighty angel who asks loudly,

> **Revelation 5:2 "… Who is worthy to break the seals and open the scroll?"**

Then we are told that no one on earth or in heaven could open the scroll, because no one was found worthy. Before we go further, remember how kingly documents were sealed? Only the party that the document was sent to was supposed to open it or read it. Usually, the receiving party was someone of importance. So we can say that unless a person was "worthy," or in other words had earned the respect of the person sending it, they could not open it. Here in Revelation, John begins to weep, because no one was found worthy. John must have had some feeling, at this point, that what was in the scroll was incredibly important. While John was experiencing what seems to me like overwhelming sadness, one of the elders (who had laid down their crowns before God's throne), tells John not to weep. He tells John to look and see that there is one who has been found worthy to break the seals and that person is "the Lion of the tribe of Judah, the Root of David …" Now, this may not be clear to first-time readers, but it's not a mystery that this is a description of the Messiah, as he was described in the Old Testament – and we know who the Messiah is (as told in the New Testament): Jesus Christ. Actually, Christ is the Greek word for Messiah. Verse 6 gives us further clarification of who this "Lion" is because John then sees a lamb that looked like it had just been killed. The surprising thing is, this slain lamb is standing in the center of God's throne. Now, I don't know about you, but my thought here is that God does not share his throne with anyone. Even earthly kings just don't let other people sit on their thrones. So, we can rightfully deduce that this slain lamb is either equal to God or is the essence of God himself. For me, if this doesn't prove Jesus' divinity, then few other things could.

One reminder here: What John sees are symbols of reality and not actual persons. He is not likely seeing God as he is, and Jesus is being represented by images here. The real, in-person Jesus, may actually be right by John, showing him these things. Jesus is showing events and characters as symbols, so John can understand the bigger picture of what happens in the visionary experience he is about to encounter. To show John how he (the Messiah) fits into the events being shown, Jesus shows him an image of himself that is a slain lamb with seven horns and seven eyes. At this point, our mental alarm should go off and we should pull out our RID rules. This picture of Jesus is very odd and scripture has not revealed Jesus exactly in this manner before (at least that I could find). Normally, we could go searching for other passages that reference this imagery or description (second rule of RID), but fortunately, we are told what these symbols mean. The last part of verse 6 says,

> **"He had seven horns and seven eyes, which are the seven spirits of God sent out into all the earth."**

Okay, by now, you may be wondering about the seven spirits. Does God have seven spirits? Well, you know what? Nowhere else in Scripture is there talk of seven spirits. Some Bible scholars believe this reference should more accurately read "sevenfold spirit," instead of seven spirits, but God does not explain this anywhere in Revelation or anywhere else in the Bible. So, our third rule of RID guides us to say, if God didn't explain it, then it is supposed to remain a mystery.

The Witnesses

Since we are merely sampling texts in this book, let's see how to apply our Fresh Read (RID) method to the two witnesses that are mentioned in Revelation, chapter 11.

As we look at the third verse of chapter 11, we read that John is told about two witnesses. What he sees are two olive trees and two lampstands. You may read this differently, but it seems very plain to me that Jesus is saying these objects represent the two witnesses. Does this, then, mean the two witnesses are simply symbolic? I suppose it's possible, but for there to be symbols within symbols does not seem to be typical when compared to what we have read so far. For now, let's assume the two witnesses are real and exist in our real world. Are they real people? Two groups of people? An ideology? At this point, we can't be sure, so let's read on. The power given to these witnesses is quite incredible, but just because the witnesses may be real, the deeds they do may be symbolic and not literal. For instance, from a non-believer's view, a person dying by God's hand may have just died weirdly. If a disease is sent by God to punish a civilization, prophecy might say God was going to send fire to their bellies. When the event occurred, the disease may have just involved terrible stomach pain – not any flames. So we need to be careful not to fill in more than what we are told. We can deduce that the enemies of these two witnesses were "devoured," which to me means they were destroyed in some manner.

Second rule of RID: Let's see if these two witnesses show up anywhere else in scripture. Do a search for "witness" or "witnesses" in your digital Bible and see what pops up. You're going to get a lot of search results, so be patient and just page through them until you find two witnesses that seem to have significance symbolically.

BAM! I found something and it's a passage I never considered before. Look at Deuteronomy 4:26-27.

> **"I call heaven and earth as witnesses against**
> **you this day that you will quickly perish from**
> **the land that you are crossing the Jordan to**
> **possess. You will not live there long but will**
> **certainly be destroyed. The Lord will scatter**
> **you among the peoples, and only a few of you**

**will survive among the nations to which the
Lord will drive you."**

This scripture may or may not apply to the witnesses in
Revelation, but I find it intriguing because Moses is telling
Israel that if they don't do what God has told them, they will be
destroyed (as a nation) and that few of them will survive.
When we look at Revelation and the terrible things that are to
happen on earth, the imagery is similar. When we see that the
temple in Jerusalem is overrun by Israel's enemies, we can
rightfully deduce that Israel, and specifically the city of
Jerusalem, are included in the devastation that is coming. In
Deuteronomy, the witnesses that testify against Israel are
"Heaven and Earth." The reason this is interesting to me is that
much of the destruction that John sees in his revelation
involves events in both Heaven and Earth. It's almost like the
two of them come against mankind to bring testing or
judgment. Now, there's no solid link we can see in either book
that helps us determine whether these two passages are related
- so for now, we are left with more questions than answers.

Two Lamps and Two Olive Trees

John is told that the two witnesses are also "two olive trees"
and "two lampstands." If we're responsible scholars we need
to do more searches, but truthfully, I found no place in
scripture that mentions two lampstands. Other places mention
lampstands but they may or may not correspond to these. We
do have the seven lampstands that stand for the churches John
is to write to. Could two of these churches be the witnesses?
Maybe; but this is more speculation than proof. There are also
lampstands in the Old Testament that are articles of the

Temple, however, I don't see much useful meaning to those here. You may find more information in your studies.

Lampstand connections were not much of a home run when we did a casual search, so let's move on to the Olive Trees. You may find different passages than I, but I locked into Zechariah 4:1-3.

> **Then the angel who talked with me returned**
> **and wakened me, as a man is wakened from**
> **his sleep. He asked me, "What do you see?"**
> **I answered, "I see a solid gold lampstand**
> **with a bowl at the top and seven lights on it,**
> **with seven channels to the lights. Also there**
> **are two olive trees by it, one on the right of**
> **the bowl and the other on its left."**

Here we find two olive trees and they are by a gold lampstand. There do not seem to be two of the lampstands but the imagery is strikingly similar. At first, Zechariah wasn't told what these olive trees/branches represent, but when we read more, we find this in the 12th to 14th verses:

> **Again I asked him, "What are these two olive**
> **branches beside the two gold pipes that pour**
> **out golden oil?" He replied, "Do you not**
> **know what these are?" "No, my lord," I said.**
> **So he said, "These are the two who are**
> **anointed to serve the Lord of all the earth."**

In these verses, we see there are two gold pipes for pouring oil. These provide the oil for the lampstands, so I find this interesting as compared to our text in Revelation. More to the point, though, is how Zechariah asked twice what the olive trees were. Obviously, he believed they were symbols that represented something and that they were not just trees. The messenger in Zechariah finally tells him that the trees represent two "anointed" persons/beings that serve the Lord. This is a little vague to us, so you will need to dig deeper and see if you can find some clues as to who these anointed persons/beings could be. One glaring possibility would be Jesus, himself. After all, He is described in more than one place (in The Bible) as the "anointed one."

The witnesses in Revelation could be symbolic of Christ and other figures, just as John the Baptist or the Apostles. These witnesses also could be symbolic of instruments of God such as the church, prophets, or other entities. The problem we have here is that we can speculate all day long and not know for sure. If you will allow me to cheat the rules for one important point, I'd like to give you a little outside information. Great scholars have been trying to resolve this for centuries and some are emphatic in their views, but the experts don't agree and no explanation is a slam dunk (at least in my view). So, we need to employ our third rule of RID. Don't play God. God does not explain who these witnesses are and they very well could be none of what the experts say. So, since God didn't tell us, we will have to be satisfied with just their existence and their mission and focus more on what effect they have on the world, rather than who they are.

Beast?

What is this "beast in verse 7 of chapter 11? It's described as one who has "come up from the abyss." It overcomes the witnesses and kills them. This is God's plan because we know that God certainly has the power to save his anointed ones and he has shown his willingness to do this. You may deduce what you wish, but for me, I think I will stick to the idea that the witnesses are defeated as part of God's overall design. The odd thing to me is the mention of this beast, almost as if we are already supposed to know what it is. Now, normally we would kick in our second rule and go searching, but let me save you some hard labor that may not yet be necessary. There is a beast like this that is presented later in Revelation, and it might be better to include those texts before exploring this beast further.

One important thing to see here is that the witnesses die in the same city as Jesus (see verse 8). So, there is a specific focus on Jerusalem during a testing period that Revelation talks about. Now, these witnesses lay in the street for 3 ½ days, then the Lord brings them back to life - calls them to Heaven - and they go up in a cloud.

Interjection: I might point out here that these two seem to be the only people who are truly "raptured" in Revelation. Other imagery may suggest a "rapturing" of Christians, but this passage seems to be the only specific case where people are caught up to be with the Lord.

An interesting point here is that the city of Jerusalem seems to be overrun for 3 ½ years and the witnesses are dead for 3 ½ days. Could these days symbolize years? Possibly, but there doesn't seem to be a precedence to change the time frame, since the other time frames in this chapter seem to be literal.

A Final Mystery

There are many mysterious things presented in Revelation. Some are clearly explained and others are not. And, no, we do not have to figure out what all of them are. Someday it will all be clear. If you would like to see the whole study of Revelation, consider my other book, REVELATION WITHOUT INFLAMMATION. In that book, I use the RID method to show what Revelation says and what it does not say. I go through all the chapters, but not every verse. It is, however, a more in-depth tutorial on the nuts and bolts of studying Revelation, without all the hype.

Before we leave Revelation, I want to leave you with a riddle that you can try to figure out yourself, using the RID method.

A Change of Scenery

Up to chapter 21, John has been seeing a lot of destruction. In fact, Hollywood couldn't orchestrate better epic destruction and general mayhem than the scenes described in Revelation. John has just witnessed scenes that are commensurate with the most action-packed, globally destructive, superhero movie you could ever see. Then, when it climaxes on earth, people are gathered to a great judgment throne where everyone must account for their evil actions and attitudes; none the least of which is refusing to repent of evil and recognize God as God. However, beginning in Chapter 21, there seems to be a complete paradigm shift. What John is shown are a new heaven and a new earth and this isn't new as in a different place; it's new as in "replaced," because John writes that the first heaven and first earth had passed away. He also adds something unexpected: There was no longer any sea. As a side note here, since John still seems to be seeing symbolic images, is the lack of a sea, mean there is no water, or does this sea represent people? Does this new earth have no people, yet? The bottom line here is that it seems there is no other way to interpret this except that God is showing John everything will be renewed. As you read this, you may pick up other things as well or have a different view, but for me, I see little mystery with the overall idea of renewal. The specifics and time frame can be discussed to no end, but the fact that there is a God-planned renewal for the "world" sometime after John was shown the Revelation, is pretty undeniable.

Now, here is an interesting tidbit. Perhaps this text and idea are not odd, but we can still use our second rule of RID to see how this idea ties into other scripture. I encourage you to do some digital searches and see just what pops up about the renewal of this earth. Without deep searching, there is one thing Jesus said to his disciples when Peter asked him what there would be for them (Matthew 19:27-28).

> **Peter answered him, "We have left everything to follow you! What then will there be for us?" Jesus said to them, "I tell you the truth, at the renewal of all things, when the Son of Man sits on his glorious throne, you who have followed me will also sit on twelve thrones, judging the twelve tribes of Israel.**

So, Jesus had already told John before that there would be a time when everything would be renewed. How glorious this moment must have been for John when he saw a glimpse of what that new earth would be like.

Bride

Again, we see and hear of a "bride" and it is the "New Jerusalem" that comes down out of heaven. Now, this doesn't say it necessarily is Jesus' bride - it just says it has been prepared as a bride. So is this just a metaphoric statement or can it be that this New Jerusalem is actually a representation of the body of Christ - that is, the church? I can tell you, you may not ever fully convince everyone, no matter what your view, because this is yet another one of those highly debated objects. What you need to do is be convinced in your own mind, after careful study and significant prayer. If there is no solid answer, then let it go and let it be something God has not fully explained.

One possible argument I might make here follows this reasoning: Israel at one time was like God's bride. He loved her, as a nation and as a people. He took care of her for hundreds of years, yet she turned her back on God, over and over. In so many scriptures, God said she had been unfaithful and had committed adultery against him. He also typed her a harlot. Then, when God sent Jesus to Israel, they rejected him as their Lord. It appears that Jesus then established the body of believers as his new bride. From that point on, the Bible only talks about this new bride and doesn't talk about Israel (Judah) as a nation or as a people becoming that bride again (except in Christ, as believers). Since the original Jerusalem was where the temple was and was called Mt Zion and The Holy City, etc., it was a spiritual embodiment of what God considered his bride. It was the center of the nation and thus represented all that they were. However, here in Revelation, it would not fit any other scriptures if this is a new city for Israel; and the picture of it being prepared as a bride, would also not fit very well. Thus, for my first read, I need to say that this Holy City is also closely tied to or embodies the church of Jesus Christ. This does not mean that I am asking you to think or believe the same way. After all, no matter how you view this text in Revelation, your walk with Christ will not likely be affected.

A Note

I want to remind you again, that most of Revelation consists of symbolic visions. What John sees is not a video viewport into the future. It is not what is happening in real time. It is a lot of symbolic creatures and objects that are doing things. These represent events in God's overarching plan for mankind. In Revelation, we see what appears to be global destruction. There is talk of the world, nations, and kingdoms. However, if we do a side search for terms like "world" and "nations," we are going to see some ideas in scripture that change our thinking completely. I encourage you to especially look at prophetic terms in the book of Isaiah. "World" and talk of everything being destroyed, cannot mean the whole planet in many of those other prophecies. Destruction and the end of the world, in Old Testament prophecies, was a reference only to the land of Israel, and sometimes its neighboring countries. Culturally, Israel was the whole world to its citizens. If Israel was gone, then everything was destroyed. And, God talked to them this way. So, when we see the text at the end of Revelation that talks of the renewal of everything (after what appears to be destruction), perhaps this is a renewal of God's relationship with Israel. The old Israel is gone and the new Spiritual Israel, born by Christ's blood is born. Adorned and ready as a bride for Christ. One clue we have that the world is not all destroyed, or that all evil persons are gone, is that when this new bride-city comes down to earth, no vile person can enter. So, if every person was destroyed by the new heaven and earth, then why would there be any vile persons?   Hmm. So, go forth and study, and see if you can solve these mysteries, without twisting or manipulating scripture.

Chapter 12

Be Prepared

Once, I heard a man say that he would never be involved in Apologetics because he would never apologize for the Gospel of Christ. To that, I had to say, hmm. I understand the confusion, but sometimes statements like this lead me to believe that many Christians today may be clinging to ideas and misconceptions that are as far away from the truth as black is from white.

A few weeks ago, I saw a video of an Islamic teacher debating with a Christian apologist. I did not see the whole debate, but the part I did see was interesting. The Islamic man was trying to make a case for Christ never having been crucified. He argued that the person who was crucified looked like Jesus, but it was not him. He used some Biblical texts to persuade the audience that when Jesus went to his disciples after the crucifixion, it was to tell them that he was alive, and not dead – nor had he been dead. So, instead of Jesus saying to his disciple, "Be happy, I have risen from the dead," the Islamic man claimed that Jesus was saying, "Be happy, because I never died." Of course, this violates so many scriptures in the Bible, it is hard to count them all. The Islamic man seemed to claim that all the teachings of Jesus' followers were based on a huge lie, and yet, all of those who would have known it was a complete fabrication, suffered a lot and became martyrs for that lie. Would any group of people do that? Perhaps a few crazies might, but everyone who followed Jesus? There is so much that could be said in defense of Jesus' actual crucifixion, and so much detail. There were so many eyewitnesses. So defending the position that Jesus actually died, is pretty easy.

No Apologies

One thing that Apologetics does not do is apologize for anything. Yes, I know that the words are similar, but the meaning is quite different. Here is what the Merriam-Webster Dictionary says about Apologetics:

1. Systematic argumentative discourse in defense (as of a doctrine)

2. A branch of theology devoted to the defense of the divine origin and authority of Christianity

So, as you see, there seems to be no sense of "I am sorry," in this process of defending the Gospel.

Here is something many Christians do not seem to grasp: It is every believer's duty to defend the Word of God. To do this, every believer should be properly equipped and willing to do it. Does this ability to present a defense of scripture come from a complete refusal to read the Bible? No. But, unfortunately, this is America. Extremely few American Christians read the Bible. What little bit of the Bible they know comes from fluffy sermons and social media memes. Is this a good way to absorb and understand the Word of God? I think the answer is obvious: no. Here is the real kicker: Many people who rarely, if ever, read the Bible, spend countless hours reading novels, textbooks, magazines, online articles, and more. So, why is the Bible never picked up? Maybe because it is not in a novel format. After all, it probably reads more like a history book. But, then, why don't people who love history read it? Maybe because to them it is more of a teaching reference? Hmm.

Here is my take on all this: I truly believe that people do not read the Bible because they have a problem relating to what it says. For instance, how do I in the twenty-first century relate to some people who I do not know and are not my relatives, who came out of Egypt, marched across the desert for forty years, and then settled in another country? Why do I care about countless prophecies that were given about these people? Why read some letters that were sent to middle-east churches during the first century AD (after Jesus' ministry)? Maybe these are all good questions – and maybe they deserve an answer. But, for the sake of this book, for now, I would just like to point out that unless a person has a close relationship with the one who authored the Bible, it will have little value outside salvation itself. To me, this is very sad. In a real sense, the Bible is a love story of epic proportions. God loved mankind so much that he sent his son to die for them. The Bible tells how God made us in the first place, and how we as a species, pulled away from God and did terrible things. It also tells about how God worked with a race of people who were the offspring of a man (Abraham) that was called God's friend. God honored that friendship to nearly ridiculous measures. He went out of his way to protect the children of Abraham and even to discipline them, so they would not kill themselves. He sent his son as a sacrifice, so all their atrocities were paid for. Then he offered the same deal of salvation and forgiveness of sins to all nations. The details of this story are many and worth reading over and over. Why? Because in the pages that tell this story, we see the character of the one we love and who loves us. We come to love him deeper when we see and hear all that he was willing to do. We also see how we can better our relationship with him and how we should live to please him. So, why should we read it over and over? Let's just be honest here. There are over one-thousand pages and 66 different books. No person I know can remember all that, no matter how many times they read it. Thus, we need to keep re-reading it. And you know what? Every person I have ever talked to, whether lay workers or ministers, has said they see something new every time they read it. So, I have to say, read the Bible every day. You do not have to read a lot at one time. In fact, it is probably better if you do not. Your retention will be better if you read a small amount at each sitting. Remember, it is not a race. There is no time standard for completing a reading of the whole Bible. Take your time. And you do not have to read it in the order it is compiled. Want to know a secret? The Bible books are not placed in the order they were written or even in sequential time periods. The Bible books are grouped by their type. The history books are mostly together - the poetic books are grouped - and the prophecies are grouped. And let me tell you, those prophecies were done over many years and under many different kings.

The Value of RID in Apologetics

What is Apologetics? As we discussed earlier, it is essentially defending the Christian Faith. It is relaying what you believe, based on scripture. It is also helping others see where their beliefs differ and where there are errors. But, the primary goal of Apologetics should never be to prove you are right. It is to win another person to Christ.

According to a document available at "equip.org" (Christian Research Institute), the ten commandments of Apologetics are as follows:

1. Gospel First, Apologetics Second

2. Stay with the Essentials

3. Remember Your Goal

4. There is More Latitude in Apologetics than in Theology

5. Find out the Real Problem

6. Avoid Distractions

7. Know What You Believe

8. Know What Unbelievers Believe

9. Do Not Be Intimidated

10. Keep the Right Attitude

Now, on the website, you can find a more detailed explanation of these commandments, but for our purposes, I think you get a general idea of what to do and what not to do. What I am not going to do in this book is teach you Apologetics. If I started into that, it would be a whole other book. So, if you all can accept the idea of Apologetics and some basic rules, then we can proceed with some simple suggestions regarding the use of the RID method of study.

First, not all people you meet will accept RID as a valid study method. This is okay. Not everyone needs to agree. RID is not a fool-proof, nor all-inclusive way to study God's Word. It was designed to provide the novice with easy tools to weed out obvious doctrinal errors. So, let's say it is a good starting place. In deep debates, it may only carry so far.

Here is my experience: When I lean on the RID method during Biblical debates, it tends to lead me toward the second Apologetics commandment: Stay with the essentials. RID tends to drive me back to what is basic. So, why is this so important? Well, let me lay that out for you. Some scholars spend countless hours trying to prove intricate arguments – especially when it comes to end-times studies (Eschatology). Portions of verses that sound like they belong with others are interwoven to create a lathwork of ideas. Now, if these were left as possibilities or ideas, they might be okay. What I mean is that we can look at the Bible with great wonder and curiosity and still be just fine in our doctrine, but when we take our musings, create doctrine around them, set them in stone, and then go to great lengths to insist that our musings are correct, we can end up with some very damaging doctrine – even though our intentions may be good.

What I find as a common doctrinal defense tactic, is quoting one verse that supports a theory, then using that as a lead for including other verses that chain together. Seems like a solid strategy, right? Well, it is not. There is a big difference between pointing out two texts that obviously say the same thing and two texts that could be interpreted several different ways, then demanding they support the same idea. For instance, if I want to establish the virgin birth of Christ, I can find specific scriptures that say Mary had not been with any man before she became pregnant with Jesus. Specific follow-on texts from the Apostles also clearly teach the same thing.

Now, if I claim I know when Jesus actually took his throne as king. I need to prove that by specific scripture. If I quote a verse that simply talks about Jesus being king, and then say the text shows the exact time when he first sat on his throne, the argument does not work. The quoted verse may or may not say that. The person using the verse can call for an interpretation that is not demanded by the actual text – especially when compared to the original manuscript and its language. However, when the given verse is challenged, another verse is given to prove that the idea is right. This chain goes on and on, building one verse in another, all the time with the assumption that the first verse was right (or at least some of the given verses are correct). However, this does not prove anything. In essence, it becomes avoidance. We must assume in a debate that the most solid information is given first and then the supporting evidence surrounds it. If the support for a position is scattered and each piece does not truly rest on a solid foundation then it is a "house of cards." If you take one shaky piece out, the whole thing collapses. So, when you see these kinds of arguments, avoid them like a plague. Stick to simple concepts and simple doctrines. The main things in God's Word are very plain. When you become embroiled in arguments where you have to put ten scriptures together to form a doctrine, and each text does not clearly state the position, it is likely not a solid doctrine. It is questionable, and can easily be challenged. When defending your faith, look for verses that plainly state what you believe. Give one or two other verses that also clearly state the same thing. If that is not enough of a foundation for your belief, then try to discuss a different aspect of your faith. Endless arguments prove nothing. If the person you are speaking to has endless online videos and lectures they want you to listen to, to prove that their intricate theories are correct, I would suggest that you just go back to your Bible and not waste your time. Anyone can talk on a video. It does not make them an expert in anything. Many people can build very convincing cases for some very false doctrines. Because a speaker is very charismatic or sounds like he knows what he is talking about, does not mean he is teaching the truth. This is why so many people have been led astray to non-Christian cults and into teachings that are not Biblical. The Bible says it or it does not. If you have to dig deep to find an extremely important doctrine, you probably missed what the original writer was trying to say. This is why we go back to RID. Read it, freshly, every time. Don't interject things. Look for the plain truth. It is there, on the page. Since it is an older language, and there is some symbolism in places, look up the words and symbols in other places to get a better idea of what the symbols mean. And, some things will be a mystery that you may never solve. The main things, however, are plain.

Courtesies

The last Apologetics commandment is "Keep the Right Attitude." This is a very important aspect of defending what you believe. If we become snarky or attack a person's character, we have lost the battle. When debating, we need to always remember what our Bible instructs:

> **Colossians 4:5-6 Be wise in the way you act toward outsiders; make the most of every opportunity. Let your conversation be always full of grace, seasoned with salt, so that you may know how to answer everyone.**

> **2 Timothy 2:23-26 Don't have anything to do with foolish and stupid arguments, because you know they produce quarrels. And the Lord's servant must not be quarrelsome but must be kind to everyone, able to teach, not resentful. Opponents must be gently instructed, in the hope that God will grant them repentance leading them to a knowledge of the truth, and that they will come to their senses and escape from the trap of the devil, who has taken them captive to do his will.**

So, respecting the person you are debating is not just a social nicety, it is a direction from God's Word.

My Experience

I have been, and currently am (as of the writing of this book), a participant in several Eschatology study groups, and I have noted that there are several different personalities in these groups. There are some that just present scriptures to support their position, while others are always posting links to videos of lectures. I do not like videos. You cannot debate with a video. It is a one-way conversation. Now, I am sure video lectures have some value, but they tend to lean toward persuasion through a presentation. What do I mean by this? Well, if the lecturer has a charismatic mannerism or talks quite fast, and with great enthusiasm, the average person is going to be caught up in the emotion. If the lecturer sounds like he fully believes what he is saying and is enthusiastic about it, he sounds believable. People get caught up in his enthusiasm and are easily swayed by his way of thinking. This is salesmanship and it is used to sell anything from soap to your next automobile. Thus, what makes a person believe in their point of view does not have to be the scripture itself, or even the structure of the argument. The "sale" is based on presentation.

When we are defending the faith, we are defending the Bible, and our doctrinal beliefs – not our way of life, or how our local church operates. In essence, we say we belief X, because the Bible says X. We do not need to rant or rave. Either the Bible clearly states what we believe or it does not. And if it does not, then we need to adjust our beliefs to align with the Bible, not the other way around. We do not bend the scripture to make it say what we believe. We bow to scripture and bend our minds and hearts to what the scripture says.

As I said previously, doctrines or arguments that are built on a house of cards should not be seriously entertained. If no single verse or contiguous passage (on its own) can clearly establish a doctrine, then question it. If it takes 10 verses from different locations in the Bible to establish a doctrine, question it. If there is a text that could be interpreted in different ways and a teacher is saying it absolutely must be one way, then question it.

In the study groups I have been involved in, many people paint elaborate word-murals to prove their position. Now, my hat is off to them for their many hours of study and their creativity, but in the end, it is still just another opinion. Many or most of the texts used to prove their "solid" points are interpreted differently by others who have studied just as hard. What seems to escape many scholars is this:

Just because you can make a case for a doctrine, does not mean it is correct.

You can work very hard and think you have a slam dunk case that certainly no one can refute, and it can be torn apart in minutes by another scholar. So, we need to not play God (RID rules) in Apologetics either. We will never know everything. God has never given all knowledge to anyone, but Christ. And, we are not him. So, what is our best course? Keep reading the Bible, but each time we do, we read it like we have not seen it before. We look for God to speak to us in new ways, about things in our lives. We keep looking up things that are not very clear, using all the tools in our Bible study toolbox. When we cannot clearly see what a text means, then we leave it as a mystery – at least for that time. If God wants us to know, he will show us the meaning – maybe in other scripture.

Now, here is the real booger: When debating in these end-times groups, I sometimes run across people who are just not very civil. Some of them revert to personal attacks. They will question your intelligence, and your ability to truly absorb what the Bible says. In some cases, a person will claim that there is no way you can be saved and a true child of God if you do not believe in end-times prophecy the way that they do. When I run across this attitude, I just shake my head. I know without a doubt that the doctrine of salvation is built on what Christ did at the cross and not on what I believe about his second coming. In fact, if I was to get very crass, I might say that a truly born-again Christian could believe Jesus is going to return in a purple bunny costume and take us all to paradise in an Easter basket! And guess what? The Christian would still go to heaven to be with Jesus when he dies. Why? Because our belief in Christ surrounds his sacrifice for our redemption, not the manner of his return.

I am going to say it again, and who knows, I may say it more, later: When you are arguing for your faith, be respectful. Never attack a person's character. On rare occasions, you might ask about a person's credentials, but I am reluctant to even go there. Stick to the Bible text, and force the Bible to defend itself. It can stand the heat. It will come out as pure gold if it is truly God's message.

End it All

If you are not in a formal debate, where there would be time limits for each point, then your discussions can go on for a very long time. In social media formats, the viewpoints can go back and forth for days or even weeks. Now, if you like this kind of unlimited debate, then go for it, but I question its value. From personal experience, I have noticed that people have a limited number of rockets in their Apologetics arsenal. Once they have fired them all, they have no more unique weapons to use. So, listen to what they say and consider their points. Weigh them against what you believe, but mostly weigh them against what you know about Biblical text and doctrine. If you question their arguments and see flaws in their arguments (in light of scripture), you do not need to tell them they are wrong. Those types of statements get you nowhere. Remember, you are persuading, not correcting. Give solid scriptures that bring a different perspective to what the other person is saying. Ask them questions about certain aspects of their arguments.

After both you and your opponent have laid out your case, a little review does not hurt, but be cautious about just saying "yes it is," and "no it isn't." This level of argument is childish and it accomplishes nothing. Be wise. Look for the point in the discussion where nothing new is being presented, and you are mostly just rehashing everything that was already said. When you reach that point, in your discussion, then stop the debate. Simply tell the other person that you cannot agree with their viewpoint, so you are agreeing to disagree. Tell them you have decided to move on to other discussions. And, do this very nicely and kindly. Thank them for taking so much time to lay out their beliefs. If it looks like they have personally compiled charts, graphs, or other documents that support their belief, you can tell them that you recognize how much work they have put into research and that you respect their hard work and commitment to God's Word. Then smile (emoji) and thank them - then move on.

Chapter 13

Arrogance: A Deadly Trap

I have told this little story before, but it seems to fit this topic, so I will repeat it.

Mrs. God

Envision a small rural community located across the bay from Seattle. Now, focus your attention on a medium-sized charismatic church and set your mental time machine to several years ago. It's a Saturday morning and my friend and I are about to embark on a major sound system upgrade in the church sanctuary. We have the ladder, wire cutters, drill, and several other tools for removing huge speakers from a ceiling beam, about 20 feet from the floor. The plan was to move the speakers from their high perch to about 12 feet from the floor and hang them on chains, thus providing less echo and better sound for people who sit toward the front of the sanctuary. We knew it would be a challenging task and also that some in the church might question the move (though the experts claimed it would make a significant difference - and it did). Needing some serious concentration for this "high-wire" task and not wanting to engage in discussions about the why's of the operation, we had hoped that no one would be in the church building this day. My friend assured me it was unlikely anyone would be there, except for possibly the pastor. These were false hopes: While setting up, we discovered there were a couple of other people downstairs that we were soon to encounter. Now let me pause here for a minute, and say that it was not my church. I did not attend there, nor did I know most of the people who did. This was my friend's church and I was just assisting the operation as a technician and sound reinforcement consultant. This is important for you to know to fully appreciate the situation as I relay the rest of the story. As we worked, a lady came up the stairs from the basement. She was about 30 feet from where we were working but her voice was both loud and prominent. She had the tone and the air of one who was in charge and who was used to getting her way. Her noticeably obnoxious manner was more intense than any I'd encountered before, and I said to myself (and then quietly to my friend), I think I just met "Mrs. God." It was flippant and unkind, but it hit a funny bone inside of me and I couldn't help but laugh to myself over the thought of God having a wife and what she might be like (not like this woman). Despite the distraction, we finished the task with only a couple of scary high-altitude moments and the sound system was significantly improved. But what about "Mrs. God?" Well, I never did discover who she was, but since that time I've joked about the situation on several occasions. Personally, whether a person is male or female I think none of us (as Christians) should sound so overbearing and demanding that we appear to be taking on God's duties.

Power Trends

Throughout history, many people have tried to grab power. Of course, world leaders who rise to power are obvious, but in every community and most organizations, some less prominent people are following similar goals. So let me ask this question:

Why do people need to be in control?

It seems to me that people look for ways to influence the situational outcomes of their lives. In America, there is so much wealth, and so many opportunities, that this is a real possibility. Most people in America have much more power over the outcome of their lives than those living in much poorer countries. Unfortunately, this leaves somewhat of an illusion that we can control every part of our lives. The uncomfortable truth is that this whole scenario is more illusion than reality. We actually have very little control over our world. We can move somewhat freely within its boundaries, but we don't truly control it. We can have some fairly minor influences on the general timeline of our future, but there is an all-seeing God that is ultimately in control. When he says yes, then it is so – and when he says no, nothing moves. Within this larger scheme, God allows us to make choices for our lives, but it is never outside his watchful eye. This brings us to a follow on question:

Why do people chase this illusion of control so relentlessly?

I think when people feel hopeless or feel like they have no control over their future, they become afraid; and when people are afraid they get desperate. And, what does desperation bring? It produces a mindset where you will try anything; even things that are not logical and not likely to succeed.

Application

So, how does this all apply to Apologetics? Though it may be obvious to some, let me try to lay it out for you. If you spend a lot of time, reading and studying God's Word, you will begin to know things that the common pew-sitter does not know. You will see connections between core Biblical ideas and their associated scriptures in a more clear light. This broader view and depth of knowledge build a doctrinal structure that can be formidable. When someone asks you questions about your faith, you have good answers. Even when tough questions are asked, it is easier to call up associated scripture that addresses the subject. And, when you are discussing your faith with other believers, you can effectively debate doctrines and personal beliefs. All in all, you are much more equipped to handle Biblical issues. However, there is a flip side to this situation. Once you gain this more broad knowledge of the Bible, you will also gain confidence. Confidence is good, but as the Bible says "knowledge puffs up." When we begin to see that we know a lot about the Bible, we can become prideful. When pride enters in, we get a feeling of "ownership." In a real sense, we think that we own what we know. This ownership is similar to what artists experience when they create a piece of art. Because they made it and thus, own it, they are proud of it.

This pride disallows them to see its flaws, and unless they can see the flaws, they cannot improve.

A friend of mine who has been a very good artist for a long time told me that when she was taking a sculpting class she experienced a significant lesson about this. She created a very nice sculpture of a human figure and was proud of it. She was bursting with pride when the instructor came around to view his students' projects, but instead of praising her for her fine work, he took the sculpture and threw it on the floor. Both the sculpture and the artist were destroyed. But, her instructor looked at her and said that unless she stopped owning what she made, she would never become truly great. She had to be willing to part with what she made. She had to be even willing to throw it all away and start over. She needed to always think in terms of "I can do better." Her instructor wanted her to see that no matter how good she got in her career, she should always look for ways to improve.

Writers have a similar problem. What they write, they own, and when they own, they cannot proofread. This is why we depend on proofreaders. No one can effectively proofread their own material. Recent knowledge of the material content makes the writer's mind fill in the gaps automatically, and provides an auto-interpretation that cannot perceive the untold information.

If we consider these parallels, it is easier to see that when we become more intimate with scripture, we form solid beliefs that we own. We can get to that place where we just know that we know. What happens at this point? We begin to claim that we have all the right answers and that our view of scripture is the right one. We defend our views vehemently and bring out several scriptural texts that support our "has to be right" position. Because our Biblical arsenal is sizeable, we become extremely defensive. If anyone disagrees, we become arrogant. We just know that if these dummies were smart at all, they could see that they were wrong. They would see the error of their ways. At this point, we start kind of looking down our noses at them. We lift our heads high, knowing that our knowledge is far superior. We can even adopt an attitude that we need to "correct" other people's views, and when they refuse to be corrected, we can become abusive.

None of this should ever be part of Apologetics. With increased knowledge comes increased responsibility. A lot of this responsibility is to instruct gently and with respect, while always remembering that what you are presenting is the way you see it. It is not a message sent from God, it is your opinion. And, no matter how "expert" this opinion is, it is still the opinion of a flawed and sinful man.

Evangelization

Here in America, we have several techniques for evangelization. Historically, we have gone door to door, talking to people individually, and handing out tracks. We have also preached on street corners, carried crosses around, and placed tracks in various public places. We have wooed people with talk of how we loved them – though we did not even know them. We have bribed people to come to church, with the idea that they would automatically come to Christ once they heard a good salvation message from the preacher. And, good or bad, some have yelled at pedestrians passing by, and told them they were going to hell if they did not repent.

So, how effective are these techniques? Most of them, including the sermons given in church, are only about 2% effective when considering long-term commitments. Rallies, seminars, crusades, revival meetings, and most large-group evangelism do help win some souls for Christ, but they are all only about 2% effective. What is much more effective is personal evangelization. When we show that we are personally interested in a person and their life - when we take them into our life - then we have a base to work from. And, I do not at all mean to make false friends. I mean, take on a person as a real friend, and when that friendship buds, talk to them about the things you appreciate and value in life. Talks about all things, both physical and Spiritual. Do not be a salesman and never fall into the trap of trying to sell salvation. Be yourself and be honest. If you honestly love Jesus and love the relationship you have with him, then tell your friend about it. You don't have to tell him that he should do the same. If you are truly friends with this person, he will consider the value of what you have and if it seems beneficial, he will want what you have. This goes the same for all of the things you talk to him about. If you love your car and you tell him how much you have enjoyed it, he will consider buying one. If you tell him about your home or your vacation, he may want to buy a similar home or take a similar vacation. This is the nature of people and friendships. People do, naturally, look at the good things other people have and wonder how they can have the same experience. So, let me say this rather strongly: Evangelization is a life-long commitment. You are taking someone into your life, to be responsible for them and their eternal soul. If you cannot lead them to Christ, immediately, then you keep sharing your experience, for their lifetime. If you win them to Christ, then your work is not over, it has just begun. You follow up with discipling them. You help them grow to maturity and then partner with them as servants of God. Winning souls is serious business and every Christian should take it this way. We are not used-car salesmen. We don't go in for the kill, then put a notch in our belt, once we have coerced a gullible mark. Winning souls for Jesus must be open and honest, simple, and rich.

A Lesson from Kenya

While working with a local missionary in the Rusinga region of Kenya, Africa, I once asked him how he evangelized. I specifically wanted to know how he approached people in his culture. He did a lot of what Americans call "cold contact." This means that the missionary does not know the people he is talking to. He has no idea how they will react to his approach, so he is at a disadvantage. Since there are times in our American lives when we talk to people we do not know and have no opportunity to truly become friends, it is important to know the best approach to cold-contact evangelism. We can easily become offensive and close the door to an opportunity. We can also be so shy that we do not accomplish anything. Thus, I wanted to know what this quite successful missionary was doing in his own country. Though the people are of different cultures, I thought maybe I could import some of his ideas. What he told me was not what I had expected. He said in his culture, he approached people very humbly. He kindly asks them if he could talk to them about Jesus or the Gospel. He gives them the full right to say no, and if they do, he walks away. He said that in his culture, this is a must. So, I thought about this approach and saw that American evangelism as a whole is not this way. We see the most successful forwarders of the Gospel as loud preachers in a big auditorium or stadium. We praise the brash street evangelist for preaching on the street corner, and hail the courage of the person who prays loudly in a restaurant, then yells a hearty "amen" at the end of the prayer. However, this pushy, arrogant behavior does not reflect the mannerism that Jesus used when preaching the Good News.

What if we changed our tactics to those that seem so successful in Kenya? I wonder. If we approached people with kind respect and gave them the feeling that they could easily walk away at any time, maybe more people would give serious consideration to what we are trying to share with them. Maybe if we communicated our concern for them, rather than the agenda we want to push, we would make a friend, rather than a customer.

Self-Defeating

Overall, arrogance is self-defeating. It smells just like it acts and it tends to turn people away. Whether you are in a debate with another scholar or talking to someone about their eternal soul, arrogance does not win points. I can yell and degrade others. I can shout my points and take on a vehement attitude, so I can appear like the absolute expert, and yet be dead wrong. Loudness does not count - pride is a stench - and an arrogant attitude proves nothing.

> **Truth is truth, regardless of attitude, but**
> **when attitude is the carrier, then attitude is**
> **all that will be considered.**

As Christians, we are vessels that carry the most valuable truth on this planet, but we must realize that we are vessels made from clay. We are fragile and temporary. Thus, we should not think of ourselves more highly than we are. We are not even close to perfect. In fact, if there is a spectrum, we are on the opposite end of perfect. We have far more imperfections than perfections. The Bible says that in God's eyes, our righteousness is like filthy, stinky rags. Does this mean we need to see ourselves as worthless? No. Christ did not die for something he thought was worthless. What we do need, is to put ourselves in the proper light. Without Christ, we are lost and dying. We cannot save ourselves, and we cannot become knowledgeable of God's Word except by his grace. Thus, all we have seen and learned from the Bible has been because God led us there and gave us enough understanding, so we could properly study. The very brain we have and its ability to reason and learn came from God. Without that gift from him, we would know nothing and learn nothing. So, we cannot afford to be arrogant or prideful. We owe everything to God, our loving heavenly Father.

All this is why we debate with humility and respect - and we evangelize with this same attitude. We listen to other points of view on the Bible and consider what they say. We carefully offer counter-points to find the real truth. We ask probing questions that beg for good answers and then see how others answer the questions. We never stop learning and we never claim to know it all. We always, always, always, offer our doctrines on the Altar of Truth. If the doctrines are solid, they will stand in any fire. If they are not, we should let them go. Arrogantly holding onto a doctrine, because you want to believe it is not a good reason. Yes, I know it can be uncomfortable to give up a long-held doctrine, but if you see many holes in what you believe, you must consider that what you believe needs to be altered. Maybe it does not need to all be thrown out, but it may need adjusting. If you see that an opposing doctrine has more evidence and a more solid base, then you must consider that your doctrine is questionable. If you find there are big questions about any doctrine, then cease teaching it – at least until you have resolved the questions beyond a reasonable doubt.

Chapter 14

Best Way to Read the Bible

I have lived in my current home for about 9 years. It is pretty rural, so we have to take several roads and make many turns to get anywhere. There are three ways we can go to get to major stores and gas stations. One route takes us south, one west, and one north.

About three years ago, I agreed to pastor a small church that is about 3 miles northwest of our home. To get to the church, I used to travel north, using part of the same northern route we use to go to major stores. It generally goes down some pretty big hills and then follows the valley. Now, when we moved to the area it was not that familiar to me. I knew of the area and had driven through it a few times, but I had no idea which roads were the best to use. I think when we moved to the area, we looked at online maps and decided which roads were best. Until recently, I thought I was taking the fastest and most direct route to the church. There were several turns and some stop signs, but I didn't question the route, and it only took six minutes to get there. However, a few weeks ago, someone said something about them traveling up a different road. Now, I had seen a lot of cars turning onto that road and many turning off of that road, but I never explored it to see where it went. One day, when I was driving home from the church, I turned onto that road to see where it went. I was not all that surprised when I saw that it met a well-traveled road, not too far from my home. I thought, Eureka, I have found a better route! For all those years I never dreamed there could be a better and faster way to go in a northwesterly direction. This "new" road had fewer turns, fewer stop signs, and a higher speed limit.

But, guess what? Now, I am trying to break my habit of using the other road. When my wife is with me, I get involved in talking to her and place my mind on autopilot, then when we get to the crossroad where we need to go straight (old way) or turn right (new faster way), I go straight. And my wife says kindly, did you want to go this way, honey? She's such a doll. I just say, nope, I forgot again. ☺

Old Ways

Sometimes the old ways are the best. Sometimes, the old ways are just old ways. It is always good to evaluate new or different ways. The old ways may work fine for you, but you may discover an even better path, that brings you a richer and possibly a better life with Christ. When it comes to reading the Bible, there are several ways. If you are like most Bible readers, you have set a goal of a certain amount of scripture for each day. This is okay and it has benefits, but it might not be the most rewarding way to read God's Word.

What is crazy these days, is that few people ever read the Bible. They own a Bible, but it sits on a shelf gathering dust. And, if we are being very real about this situation, it is hard to believe that out of 66 books included within the covers of the Bible, a Christian can find nothing interesting to read. There is so much detail in many of the historical stories, and such intricacy in the Apostles' letters that there is no way anyone can remember it all, even if they read it a hundred times. I think this should bring us to a place where we evaluate how far our love for God goes if we just do not care about what he authored.

The one really good thing you can do is make the non-reading, be the old path. Yes, you have gone that way for a long time, but there is a better and more rewarding path. The clear truth is that we can know God better and more intimately when we read what he has written.

Methods

As I said, there are different methods of reading the Bible, but before we look at some of them, I want to make this one point clear: This is not about Bible study, this is mostly about Bible reading. Now, reading may lead you to deeper studies, but the methods I am going to discuss are more about reading than deep studies. In this book, we have already talked about how to go into the deeper studies, but if we only look into Greek passages and try to unlock some of the technical aspects of the Bible, we can become so embroiled in the mechanical study that we lose the real message of the simple words on the pages. We should always study, but even more, we need to connect to the author (God). If we focus on the principles and laws and miss God's desire to be close to us, then all our studies are useless. To me this is tragic. I have met many scholars who spend a lot of time arguing their points of view. They listen to countless videos and listen to people who agree with their point of view. Their time is spent bolstering their positions. They want to become more and more of an expert in their doctrines and make it their main goal in life. Because it all has to do with God and his Word, then they feel "spiritual," and very "Christian." After years of being buried in their apologetic practices, they lose sight of the real purpose of God's Word. It was never designed by God to be a point of contention. When the Bible divides Christians, it makes God sad. He desires us to be unified – as we are truly led by his Spirit. We are to love one another and put our Christian brothers above ourselves and our agendas. Does this mean we cannot discuss God's Word or disagree about interpretations? No. What we need to do, though, is keep that in its proper place. The discussions should never, ever, keep us from having a close relationship with our brothers and sisters in Christ.

> **If God's Word divides us, this is a tragedy,
> above all tragedies.**

Let's seek better unity in the body of Christ, and focus mostly on what we have in common, rather than engaging in spats over scriptural technicalities.

Now that I have vented on all that, let's look seriously at methods of reading God's Word.

<u>Reading the Bible in a Year</u>

One goal that many Christians have had is to read the Bible through in a year. To facilitate this, the Tyndale publishers produce a Bible that is titled, "One Year Bible." No, I am not getting anything from Tyndale, but they have been in the Bible publishing business for a very long time and seem to be a reputable company. I am sure other Bibles in the world also have guides for reading the Bible in a year, and I have seen pamphlets and workbooks that suggest certain readings for each day.

Reading through the Bible in a year is not hard if you are very faithful to the program and do not fall behind. After all, you only need to read about 3 ¼ chapters in a day to get through it all. How long does this take? Well, of course, it depends on how long the chapters are and how difficult the text is to read. If we look at how many words are in an average chapter, we can calculate this. My research shows that there are an average of about 26 verses in a chapter and about 25 words per verse. So the average chapter has around 650 words. Since the average adult reads at around 250 words per minute, you should be able to polish off an average chapter in less than 3 minutes. If you are reading 3 ¼ chapters a day, that is around 2100 words. This means you can do a day's reading in less than 9 minutes. So, can the average person spare 10 minutes a day to read the whole Bible in a year? Of course they can. Not reading a significant amount of Bible text every day, is not about time. It is not because you are too busy. It is because it is not as important as the other responsibilities and desires. So, this has to be a serious commitment upfront and a daily habit that you refuse to break.

Now, there is a flip side to this whole scenario. If we look at this whole situation realistically, sometimes life brings us emergencies. These things put us in positions where we cannot easily control our own time. So, here is the uglier side of reading the Bible in a year. It is much harder to accomplish this goal if you have to catch up. Once you fall behind in that 9-minute reading, it doubles the next day, then triples the day after. So, you can easily see that if you had just an impossible weekend where you could not read at all, you would need to read for half an hour, instead of 9 minutes to catch up. And if you were very ill, you might fall behind for a week or so. For this reason, many who have faithfully started this noble quest, have given up. Not because they could not read for 9 minutes, but because they could not face the discouragement and drudgery of catching up. So, you should take a good look at your lifestyle and your responsibilities before you commit to reading the Bible in a year. If you do want to read the Bible in a year, you can still do it, without the regimented daily portions. You can pick up the Word and read as much as you can and want to. You might read a whole book or more in one sitting, and maybe this fits your lifestyle better. Then you can skip some days and still get through it. If you are an avid reader, getting through the Bible is not that hard. The average reader needs from about 54 to 72 hours to read it all. If you believe, based on your reading times of novels, that you can easily spend this many hours in a whole year, then set this as a goal, and just work on it. If you complete it before the year, then, yay! If you get it done in 14 months instead of 12, who cares? I am sure you have not finished every novel you have ever written within the time you desired. And, I am guessing that you did not beat yourself up when you did not read a novel in the time you wanted. Everything in the Bible is important, so the more of it you read, the better, even if you finish it years later. However, please keep this in mind: It is better to know what you have read than to just read the Bible from cover to cover.

Read the Bible for content, rather than for conquered real-estate.

<u>Reading One Book Every Day</u>

Another method of reading God's Word is to read one complete book every day. Of course, if we read books like Jude, it is easy, but the book of Psalms has 150 chapters. Still, it is a good goal. One thing about reading a whole book at one time seems obvious. You are going to complete the whole Bible in a much shorter period. Compare the one-year method of 3 ¼ verses, to a whole book. Instead of 3 to 4 chapters in a day, you would be reading an average of about 18 chapters in a day. Since there are 66 books in the Bible, you could finish the Bible in just 66 days. So, even if you skipped a few days, you could easily read through the whole Bible in about 2 ½ months. Nice, huh?

Again, we look at this plan to see if it fits our lifestyle. Can we do this? If we fall behind, we really cannot catch up. We just have to take longer. Will this bring discouragement? You need to judge this for yourself. You know you. Many people have been able to do this, and many have not. If you accomplish this, it does not mean you are more spiritual. It may mean you are just more stubborn. Again, the goal of reading the Bible is to take in what it says and live it. If I am reading to just put pages behind me, then my reading may be more for pride than Spiritual benefit.

Reading a Chapter Every Day

Okay, for children and some adults, maybe reading only a chapter a day fits better with your lifestyle. This is okay. It will take much longer to get through the Bible, of course, but it is still a good idea.

When I was about 12 years old, I committed to reading one chapter every night, after I hopped in bed. Throughout my teen years, I faithfully read a chapter every night, unless I stayed overnight somewhere else. Some nights it was tough to get through the whole chapter, especially if I did not relate to what was in the chapter, but I tried hard to keep up the pace. I think it set real precedence in my life, for keeping my life grounded in Christ. Looking back, I see that there were many temptations in my teen years, but it was hard to do those things and also read God's Word every day. It was an either-or, with me. Either God was important, or doing what I knew was wrong was. For the most part, I chose God. So, even for mature adults, perhaps it helps us make the right choices in our lives, when we have our noses in God's Word, regularly.

A Better Way

The RID (Fresh Read) method of Bible study is a good basic way to weed out problems, but it is not a rigid reading style. There are other ways of reading, when it comes to nurturing your soul, daily. You may or may not do deeper studies of God's Word daily. In fact, I would recommend that unless you are teaching or preaching, you gauge your deeper studies, and use them wisely. You can pull RID out at any time and apply it as required. And, you can keep the principles in the back of your mind, until you discover issues in your daily reading, then set aside a special time to look into the problems. Never be hasty in Biblical problem-solving. Take the time to get real answers and try hard to find the answers on your own, before you look at any commentaries. Let God lead you to the answer.

Considering what I have written to this point, let me share with you something special. I want to tell you a little secret and it is about what I see as the very best reading method. Again, this is not the best study method, it is the best daily reading method.

When I was about 25 years old, I had an electronics repair shop. Because my wife had to be at work very early, she dropped me off, way before my store opened. During this time, I desired to develop a better relationship with Christ. I was beginning to do lay ministry at a local church and Jesus was becoming much more important to me. At one point, God impressed something on me that was strong and clear. He said, "I want to talk to you." To this point, I thought only super-spiritual people heard from God and everyone else had to go by signs - but this message to me was different and powerful. It was not just a thought or impression. This word came with a very powerful presence of God; the kind that you feel when God is there in a church service. What is interesting to me, even today is that I was wondering what he was going to say. Here was how God responded: He said that if he began talking right then and continued for the rest of my life that he could not tell me everything he would like me to know. I said to myself, wow. So, I listened and he showed me so many things. Among the first things he showed me was how deeply God loved me.

At about this same time, I started reading my Bible in those early morning hours, before the store opened. I would grab some breakfast food, and sit down with my Bible. I would pray and ask God to show me what I needed to know that day, then I would read the Bible and just listen with my spirit. Do you know what happened? I heard. Nearly every day, God spoke to me about my life and what I needed to do. He encouraged me and showed me more of his love. Some things were so powerful that I started writing them down and posting them in my shop for others to read when they came in. God taught me how to listen to him and how to apply what he said to my life. Do you know what affect that had on me? It transformed my life. During this period, my ministry grew and people began inviting me to go places and minister to groups of people. A few years later, God called me into full-time itinerate ministry.

So, what was a key element in this life-transforming scenario? Certainly prayer and an open heart, but it was married with a method of reading God's Word that was different than I had ever done before.

I read to hear God speak to me.

And, when I received what God was wanting me to know, I stopped. Most days, it was only about a paragraph. On rare occasions, it was a whole chapter. For a few days, there was more than one thing God wanted me to know that day, but on most days it was a single message. As my spirit was open to his, he would let me know when to stop reading, and when to keep going. One wonderful and important thing is that when I received that special word from him, it was like gold to me. It was my special nugget for that day. This is what is so important to understand: I stopped because any additional information tended to muddy that day's message to me. I didn't need or require any more than that one special message and if I pondered that message all day, it sank in and became more of my life. When I read a whole chapter, just to cover ground, there was a lot of information, but not necessarily a special message. When I slowed down and considered every word I was reading, while having my spirit wide open to him, I could more easily receive what God had for me. God's direction for my life, made me grow and bloom. It changed my life and it changed my whole concept of daily Bible reading. And, you know what? I still read this way. At least one time each day, I look for God's direction and his presence, while reading the Bible. As a pastor, I read a lot of the Bible for other things, but this one time is special and will always be.

I hope you can find this same rewarding path that I found. Please, read God's Word in a way that he can speak to you. If you are a young Christian, do read the Word in larger amounts than a paragraph, so you can become familiar with its contents. However, keep one special time aside, for an intimate time with your God and your savior. It will transform your life.

Chapter 15

An Aerial View

There's a popular southern Christian chorus that says "it's not over 'til it's over." Other than one other line in the song, I believe this phrase is just repeated. Perhaps the phrase is a tell on the song itself because the chorus is usually sung over and over - thus, you don't know when the song will be over until the song director decides to quit. What is kind of odd to me is that music directors use this song in a way that gets crowds worked up. Apparently, singing a chorus like this tends to create energy when it is done repeatedly. Though the words of the song are not specific or particularly meaningful, people assign meanings of their own and become quite excited about it. I suppose it is kind of a rallying concept, and I do have to say that it seems to work. Personally, I prefer songs that state specifics, and if it is Christian, I prefer songs that talk about God and his son, Jesus. However, if God gets glory from people singing a song, even like "It's not over 'til it's over," then let it be. Let's do that. ☺

Viewpoint

I think it is beneficial to many readers when I review all the things we have discussed. Thus, this chapter presents an overview or aerial view of this book's content. Here is where I often put in a caveat. If you think you understand and remember all the concepts in this book, then you may not need to read this last chapter. You are perfectly welcome to exit here and move on to a new book. Of course, I must recommend that you read one of mine. At this point, there are over 12 books to choose from. Okay, so now that I have inserted a cheesy advertisement, I can move on to a meaningful review.

Bad Bible Study?

It is a great thing to study the Bible, but if we do not study it in a good way, we may not get much out of it, and we might not see what the Bible is saying. So, what would a "not good" way be? Well, one way would be to just prove a point. When we look up scriptures to use against someone else, especially a brother or sister in Christ, we are not practicing the kind of unified love that Jesus desires. The Bible should never be a weapon against another believer. And, if our purpose to study the Bible serves to feed our pride, so we can prove we are right, then we have a shallow understanding of God's Word. The Word of God is not a repository of arguments. It is not a reference book of verbal weapons. It is the story of how much God loves us. Yes, we need to defend our faith, but

Apologetics launches from deep faith, not a deep need to be right. In case I am not being clear here, let me say that if you only open your Bible when you want to pull out scriptures for an argument, you do not know the Bible. Knowing or using a few key verses to support your sense of righteousness, does not make you an expert at Biblical doctrine. When you use a few choice verses and think you understand the doctrine you are touting, then you are selling yourself and your opponent short. To truly understand the doctrines of the Bible, we need to understand the heart of the one who authored them. When we see hundreds of examples of how God dealt with people, over thousands of years, then see the mannerism of Christ and all he did, we can more clearly see the scope of who God is. Then, when we read his commandments, and see his interactions with people, his expectations, and his directions and warnings to his disciples, we understand the context of what he expects of us. We understand not only the words, but also the intention behind them. True and honest Bible study seeks to know the author, not just his book.

The more obvious element of bad Bible study arises from taking our ideas into our reading. As I said, when we go into the Bible, looking to prove a point, we are not really studying God's Word. Similarly, when we go into a daily reading pattern with preconceived ideas, we also do not study God's Word. Instead, we make God's Word say what we want it to, or what we are comfortable with. This is a pattern and methodology that we do, without even thinking about it.

Fresh Read

To prevent this practice of taking our ideas into God's Word, it helps to adopt a fairly rigid set of rules for yourself. Now, these can be your own rules, and as long as they produce an honest and untainted study. For this book, we are looking at a proven method that is called "Fresh Read." The idea of Fresh Read is to try reading each passage of scripture like you have never seen it. Sound easy? It is not. In a real sense, you have to temporarily forget everything you have ever heard about the verses you are reading. You have to pretend you are a young Christian (or you would have to be one). The second part of this is similar. Since you cannot always see a text in that pure, first-time, manner, you must offer your pet doctrines on the Altar of Truth. Truth matters. Make the Bible stand on its own merit. If the doctrines are truly from God, then the Bible will clearly present them.

To aid in this Fresh Read, there are three rules you can use. These are represented by an acronym, R.I.D. (RID). This stands for, "Read it as if you had never seen it," "If it sounds weird, look it up," and "Don't play God." Let me briefly remind you of what these mean. First, you read just what is on the page and consider nothing else. You consider no other scripture. You only consider what the actual texts mean. Second, if in what you read there are odd terms or symbolic language, then look elsewhere for these terms or symbols. They may be better explained in other texts. Remember that God did not always repeat everything, and the Bible writers do assume the people they are writing to remember what God has said. Because you may not have that broad knowledge, you may have to look in earlier texts to see what God said about the subject before. A digital search of the Bible can help in finding unfamiliar terms and symbols. The last rule of RID is to not play God. This means that after you have tried to understand a Bible passage using the first two rules of RID, but still do not seem to have enough information for clear understanding, then mark it in your mind as a mystery. The truth is that many prophecies are shrouded in mystery. Is it mysterious because you are dumb or unlearned? Are you just not enlightened, as some apologists may claim? No, no, no. God said, way back in Moses' day that he speaks through prophets in riddles. So prophecies are riddles. I do not care who says they are not, the Bible says they are. Now, God explains some things in his riddles, and these things may also give us clues to other things that are not explained. Even so, there are some things he has purposely veiled. For instance, God has told us that we will not cease to exist at death, but live on forever with him if we believe in Jesus and trust him. We have a few glimpses into the afterlife, yet the details of our existence are not all that clear. So the spiritual world, the exact makeup of God, and our existence remain a mystery. It is something God has not fully revealed and he is likely not going to. All we need to do is trust him and trust that he knows how to take care of us when we die. We completely place ourselves into his hands. It takes a lot of faith and trust in someone to place ourselves in this position, but our loving God has proved to be faithful to us in our lives, thus we can also trust him with our eternal souls. We do not need it all spelled out in scripture for us to believe he has it all figured out.

It is all Greek to Me

It would be so convenient for us if the Bible had been written in English, right? Well, it was not. The majority of God's Word was written in a very ancient version of Hebrew-

Aramaic. The rest of the Bible (New Testament) was written in Koine Greek, with a few Hebrew-Aramaic words thrown in here and there. Why did the Jews who spoke Hebrew write in Greek? Because it was the business language and was known throughout the Roman Empire. In that period and region, if you wanted as many people as possible to read what you wrote, you wrote in Greek.

Having the Bible in languages that the vast majority of the world does not know, makes Bible study more difficult. Ancient Greek and even more ancient Hebrew is hard to accurately translate into modern English. And of course, English is constantly changing also. So, it does help to have some good study tools near when you are reading and studying the Word. Language interlinear books, word expository, Bible dictionaries, and more can help unravel some of the difficulties in the original manuscript.

One important thing I have discovered is what I call "parallel phrasing." This is a critical thing in translations, yet not commonly talked about it church Bible studies. Let me lay this idea out for you. Have you ever been misunderstood, when you said something? What about when you texted someone? It happens to us all. Whether spoken or written, we can say something that seems very clear to us, yet it is not clear to another person. Perhaps they were thinking about something else when they listened to your idea and it tainted their understanding. Perhaps they just generally phrase things differently. So, here is some truth about language, even when people speak the same one. A single phrase can be spoken correctly, and yet be taken in different ways. Punctuation in writing helps, but even this has its flaws.

A common example of proper punctuation issues is shown
below:

Let's eat Grandpa.

Let's eat, Grandpa.

I doubt anyone wants to be a cannibal, so the second version
seems to convey the right message. However, the words are
the same in both sentences. A tiny pause in the way you say it
or write it changes the meaning. This type of
misunderstanding and more also happens even when there are
no punctuation errors. Phrases we commonly say can often be
taken in different ways. One sentence can mean two different
things to two different people and both of these people will be
sure they have the correct meaning. So, which is right? Well,
we would have to ask the person who said it (or wrote it).
What if the person is dead? Hmm. Here is where the Bible has
a problem. The original writers are dead. The Holy Spirit can
help us, yet scholars that say they are led by God, still disagree.
So, some of them are probably off in their interpretation, but
which ones?

If we take these ideas and hold them as a reference, we can see
something about studying the Bible that is very important.
When I read a phrase in English, I take it in and decide its
meaning. If the phrase is the same or similar to the ones I have
heard or used, then I will assume that the writer of that
scripture meant the same thing as I would. And, I will not
question it, because it seems plainly stated. However, our
Bible is a translation into English from a different language
that has a different phrasing structure. Nouns and verbs are not
in the same places and tenses are far more complex, so we have

to raise this question: Though the words and phrases are correct, do they carry the common meaning that is in our current culture, or do they carry the "alternate" meaning?

Here is the reality of all this. Several times while I studied, I looked up the Greek text version, and I was easily able to see the intention of the writer (or at least some of it). I looked at the context of the subject being presented and kept the same thought flow in the verse I was studying and when I brought in the Greek, I saw how the writer was including the ideas in his writing. When I compared it to English, I saw that the translation was correct and accurate, but the phrases in English would likely be taken like a person would say them in everyday conversation, whereas the original manuscript was trying to say something slightly different. It was the alternate way to see those phrases. So, though the common English version was not wrong, doctrinally, it was a little left of what the writer intended his audience to know. When we see what the writer meant, it is often wider and deeper. Now, do you have to know Greek to do this? No. The tools (books) are available to help you with these things. These are the deeper study methods for people who want to dig in, but even as a casual reader, there are times when you will need them.

If you come across a verse that seems to contradict another one or a verse that seems to be talking about something different than the rest of the passage, go to a word expository and look up some of the words, but also go to an Interlinear Bible and see what the literal translation is, word for word. When you see how the words are used together and the meaning of the words, you will likely see what the writer was trying to say.

Very Old History

When looking at the historical books of the Bible, we see cultures that are very different from ours. Big power was always trying to get bigger and someone was always trying to take what someone else had. Religions and pagan beliefs were deeply embedded into all the nations' societies. So, events that occurred are also going to be quite different than they are today. Animal sacrifices were common and ideas about what was right and wrong were quite different than in America. Because culture and events were different, when we look into the early Bible days, we have to interpret things in this context. When we picture Abraham traveling from one place to another, we cannot put him into the context of walking on the sidewalk of New York City or riding on the subways. Neither can we visually place him hacking his way through a Jungle in South America. Thus the things Abraham did and said must be taken into this perspective. And, when God talked to him and him to God, we also need to realize the environment in which Abraham lived. Abraham's responses may have been different than our responses today. What God said to Abraham, also might be different than what God would say to us, today. God is personal and he deals with us personally. He knows how we think and how we talk. There would be no purpose in God coming to us and speaking in Hebrew. As followers of Christ, there would be no value for God to come and scream at us about our sin – sin that is covered by the blood of Jesus. God talks to us according to who we are and where we are.

It might also be good to note that the first part of the book of the Bible, Genesis, is written in a poetic format. Its language and structure seem to be different than the Law books that follow it. However, I am not an expert in this area, so if I am wrong about this aspect, I am fine with that. One thing is clear, Genesis does not give a lot of detail about how God created this world. We have a quick description of God speaking, and creative miracles happening, but little to no scientific or physicist-level explanations. So, the beginning of this earth and mankind are shrouded in about as much mystery as where we go when we die.

Lay Down the Law

Several books of the Old Testament talk about God's Law. It starts in Exodus, but there are also more pieces in the books that follow, and in Deuteronomy, Moses reminds the children of Israel of what the Law says, right before they march into the promised land. He also expands the original law, explaining how it is applied. It is very important to read and remember what this Law says, at least in general. We need to know how strict it was and which parts were more emphasized. Doing this helps us see what God hates. These are things we also can watch out for in our own lives. Now, this being said, I want to make this one point very clear: Those of us in the Kingdom of God (because we believe in Christ and his sacrifice) are not under the Law. I want to say that again. We are not under the old Mosaic Law.

When we study the Old Testament, we see references to the Law and we hear God, over and over, warning the Israelites to follow the Law. However, we need to never, never, never, get caught up in applying those things directly to our Christian walk. Out final word for how we live comes from Jesus' teaching and those who followed him as disciples. We follow

Christ, not the Law. The old Law is valuable to use as a lesson on how things used to be, and what we are set free from. When I hear preachers take a text from Isaiah, Habakkuk, or another prophet, then use it as a directive for us to comply with it or feel guilty about not complying with it, I just cringe at the misuse of scripture. Jesus and his disciples have given us clear directions on how we should live. Thus, all Christian teaching should follow this example and context. When we form doctrines and then prove their integrity, we must take this into account. We cannot afford to read Paul's letters to the new Christian churches and see how they apply to our own Christian lives, then look into the Old Testament and treat it the same way. Though we call the Bible, God's Word, we cannot view every single word in the Bible being spoken as a directive to us, personally. If we do, we will be marching around cities, going to war all the time, tearing down idols, building temples, and more. None of these apply to us as Christians. Even the doctrine of tithing is part of the old Law. It is not taught in the New Testament. Giving is definitely a part of the New Testament and it is a gracious and non-coerced giving, not a forced 10% of everything. And churches need to stop teaching tithing as a Biblical directive to us today. Besides, even if someone did want to observe the Old Testament tithing, it would be way different than what any church is teaching. To read more about this, get my book, CHRISTIANS DON'T BE SO GULLIBLE.

The Value of Songs

Some songs are pretty and some are not. Some have deeply meaningful lyrics and some are just non-sense. The Bible has many songs – well, at least the lyrics for songs. I think it would be nice if we could hear how the Psalms sounded when set to music. I also think that the sound of the original Hebrew might flow better and be prettier, than reading them in English. Even so, many of the Psalms have great meaning and flow pretty well.

So, songs can be wonderful, but of what value are they in God's Word? Well, some of them contain prophecy. Obviously, the Spirit of God was moving David and others to write things about both their "now" and "future." What was in their future? The coming of the Messiah - their ultimate king.

Besides prophetic content, we also see in the songs the aspect of sorrow and struggle. We hear men calling out to God for help and trusting in him to rescue them. So, there are great lessons for us as Christians, when it comes to being able to trust God. After all, if we cannot trust God, then we cannot trust in all he did to bring his son Jesus into this world.

Should we sing these songs today – maybe bring them into our church services? Well, many have been put to music and many have been sung in churches, though mostly they include only parts of a Psalm. Is there anywhere in the Bible that commands us to sing the Psalms? No. Is there value in singing them? Possibly. But, are we more Spiritual or closer to God because we do? No. We draw closer, because we want to, not because we sing certain songs.

The Psalms and other songs in the Bible are important, but there is no "magic" in them. They are not to be looked at as something that forces God's hand. We should not pray the Psalms, thinking that we can curry favor with God. He already loves us more than we can imagine and wants to give us what we ask. Thus, a simple and honest prayer, from your heart, has more power than anything else you can do.

Prophets and Onions

Prophetic scripture often has layers of meaning and it is certainly presented in a riddle format. So, what do we do with these texts? Here are some clues: First, try to identify the time period. If you can identify what king was on the throne or a major event, then you can go back to the books of Kings and the book of Chronicles and see what was happening. There may even be pieces of prophecy stated within the book or a mention of the prophet's name. If you want an easier way to connect the prophecies with the period, get a Chronological Bible. Why? Because the commonly used Bible is compiled by book types, not by the order they were written, or by the events described in them. The prophetic books are grouped in the last part of the Old Testament and their prophecies span quite a long period.

Within each Old Testament prophecy, God (or his angel) may explain the meaning of some of the symbols and language, but many times he does not. When we employ RID rules, we can search for terms or symbols elsewhere in the Bible, and sometimes we can get a clue as to the possible meaning of a short passage of scripture. God does repeat the same terms in his Word.

As you read through the prophetic books, keep in mind that you do not have to figure it all out. The ideas are pretty clear, regardless of the symbols. The prophecies are generally one of two types. They either promise a great and beautiful future, or a dismal future filled with destruction and sorrow. Even when we cannot pick up on all the specifics, we know that things will be good for the country or people that are mentioned, if God says so. Equally so, things will be terrible if God says so. This is an important Biblical truth for us to grasp. When God says something will happen, it will happen. For those who follow God and are obedient, there are rewards. For those who turn their back on God and serve other gods, there are terrors and disasters. Even though this is an Old Testament principle, it still holds today. Globally, God rewards those who seek him with an honest heart. Even nations who (as a whole) regard God and seek his will, God rewards. Does this mean that the promises he made to Israel apply to all other countries, in all eras? No. God only made a contract with Israel. Still, even with Abraham, we see this principle that individual people who honestly seek God are rewarded. Thus, if many people do this in a nation, and much of the leadership follows this same honest seeking, God seems to help that nation in many ways. And, if that same nation turns its back on him, they will fare no better than Israel.

One thing prophecy will never do is violate the central doctrines of the Bible. God is not flighty or whimsical. He is constant and never changes in his character, so his messages and his directions for mankind are consistent. God does not come along one day and say one thing, then come the next day and say the opposite. So, if you see a text in the Bible and it looks like it violates everything else in scripture, look at it again and dig deeper. Don't manipulate the text to make it palatable. Find out what the original manuscript says and investigate the flow of ideas. In the end, if your ideas are different than the text, bend your ideas to the text, not the other way around. You may not understand all of the purposes of the text, but align yourself with what it says.

How clear are the Gospels?

Of all the books in the Bible, you would think that the four Gospel books would be the clearest, right? I mean, these books tell of Jesus' life and of many things he said. These are critical to salvation and eternal life. So, we should be able to trust the Gospel books to tell us the straight truth, right? Hmm. Well, I suppose if I say, no, then I get labeled as a heretic, but the uncomfortable truth is that Jesus said he was hiding things. He told his disciples that he taught using parables so that people would not fully understand what he was teaching. He said he would only tell the disciples what he meant. Of course, we have those teachings now and further teachings of the disciples, so we mostly know what Jesus was saying. Thus, they are pretty clear to us, if we study well. However, there were things that Jesus told his disciples about their future that were not clear to them, and may still not be immediately clear to us. He told his disciples he was going to die, then rise again, but they didn't understand what he meant until he rose from the dead and appeared to them. Perhaps they believed that he was talking about a spiritual resurrection, like the prophets who had died before Jesus. Regardless, there was some mystery there.

In addition to the before-death information Jesus gave, he also told his disciples about the farther future. For example in the 24th chapter of Matthew, Jesus laid out some serious warnings. He told them bad things were coming, but they could escape if they looked for the signs. They listened and remembered - and when they saw the things Jesus said were going to happen, they left the Jerusalem area. The unbelievers stayed and were killed. Now, some scholars believe that this prophecy will repeat someday in some way. Is this true? Well, you have the RID rules and a Fresh Read approach to scripture, so you can run all the scriptures out to see what they say and what they do not say. When given arguments, you can read entire passages, instead of single verses, to see what is being said. In the end, after you have looked at the structure and supports of the end-time doctrines, you can determine for yourself, where the greatest weight is in scripture. If you would like some help, get these two books, REVELATION WITHOUT INFLAMMATION, and JESUS' WORDS WITHOUT INFLAMMATION.

The Followers

As important as Jesus' Words are, we cannot discount the teachings of his followers. The writings of the Apostles and major leaders of the time are very important in establishing sound Biblical doctrine.

Paul, of course, is the main contributor to New Testament writings. He penned more books than any other Christian teacher of his time. Thirteen books are positively identified as his, with Hebrews being forever in question as a possible fourteenth.

So, how do we study these books of the Apostles? Well, many of them were letters written to specific churches. They answered questions and issues of that church. So, what do we do with this information? Well, first, we realize it was not written to us. We can learn a lot from what Paul is telling a church, but we should not automatically take it as a direct command to us. For instance, if Paul says to greet each other with a Holy kiss, we do not have to do that to obey God. In some cultures, this is completely inappropriate and would bring dishonor to the church. So, when we read these letters, we can match principles with Jesus' teachings and the other Apostles. When we see consistent teaching about core Christian doctrines, we can pull these out as solid foundations for our Christian walk. We can rightfully say that this is the way Christ wants the church to be, and then apply it to our life.

This filtering of what is more cultural from what is critical and eternal doctrine can be tricky. We want to just read what is on the page and take it as it is said (except for symbolic language), but when we take it at face value, we need to also include the honesty of who the writer was writing to. If we lose sight of the target audience of the Bible, then we can easily get into false doctrines and cultish practices. Some have gone down this path and separated themselves from society, believing it was directed by scripture. It was not. So, be careful. Have some common sense. Pray earnestly. Read with an open heart, and also, use your mind.

A Work of Weeding

Weeding. Hmm. Whenever I hear this word, it just makes me cringe. There are only a few things I hate more than weeding. However, when I see my flowers being overtaken by weeds, I feel sorry for the little boogers and make a rescue plan. The idea is to save the good by removing the bad. And, guess what? The good looks much better when the bad is not choking them out. They even thrive and grow better.

Is there a parallel here, when it comes to scripture? I am sure there is. There is definitely a parallel when it comes to the Good News and the believers because Jesus used a parable about weeds to demonstrate this parallel. Other scriptures that the Apostles wrote, encourage us to rightly divide the Word and to study it to show ourselves approved. So, this weeding of scripture seems to be not only a Biblical concept but also a duty of every believer. Since we know what to do, the one question that remains is how to do it.

The RID rules are a good way to start weeding out falsehood from the truth. If we have heard many teachings about a scripture, all that stuff is floating around in our head and it can taint what the text says. Why? Because some things we have heard are pure truth and other things have been the musings of someone, based on their own life experiences or a learned doctrine. Most Christians remember teachings about doctrines that are both true and false. Christians read books, see movies, listen to radio and TV programs, and hear hundreds of sermons and teachings. The ideas contained in all these things are from different sources. There are many teachers and doctrinal bases represented in all that media. Thus, you will hear a variety of viewpoints and all that will be deposited into your memory. If none of this has been filtered at the time it entered our brains, then it remains as accepted information. Is this bad? Well, it is a fact of life. We hear stuff and we do not always have the tools or energy to completely filter things when they are flowing at full speed into our ears. The point here is that when we read God's Word, we need to install a gate between all those memories and what we read on the pages. We need to hold back the flood of correlating information in our brains and just consider what is printed on the page we are reading. For a few moments, there should be only the words in front of you, and nothing else. This a pure and Fresh Read. It gives us the best idea of what the original manuscript said and becomes a starting place for understanding what the original writer was trying to relay – without any other imposing voices. This is the essence of the "R" in the RID rules. We read it as if we had never seen it. When we believe we have the true intention of the original writer, then we can open that gate of other things we have heard, but this opening must be just a crack. Instead of throwing the protective gate wide open and letting everything flood in, we need to crack it open and just consider one position or doctrine at a time, so we can compare it to what we saw in the text. Each viewpoint we have remembered about the text needs to be carefully examined to determine whether it complies with the text.

> **We are not making the text comply with the doctrine. We are making the doctrine comply with the text, or discarding it.**

Each doctrine, then, is offered up on the Altar of Truth. The altar is what the Bible says, in its purest form, without manipulation or excuse.

So, you can see how using RID helps us rid ourselves of preconceived ideas and questionable doctrines. This is a good method to begin the Biblical weeding process. It does not require hours or weeks of study to find the truth. Instead, we let the Bible do the proving.

If the text does not clearly state the doctrine, then shelf it until you find another that does. If you find, no scripture that clearly states the doctrine, then keep it on the shelf. Over time and with study, clear your shelf of the never-proven doctrines.

Now, can the other rules of RID help in the weeding process? Yes, but perhaps to a lesser degree. The "I" is for seeing if there are odd phrases or symbols. This is very important because things that are not well defined are rich fodder for end-times theories. Yes, theories, not solid doctrines. If you can do a Fresh Read, then look for other places in scripture where symbols or terms are used, then make a pretty good determination of what the writer is trying to relay, you are miles ahead of "experts" who create an elaborate mosaic of end-times events. Let's stick to only what is written.

The last weeding tool is the "D" in RID, which stands for don't play God. Put simply, when you have done a Fresh Read and looked up odd phrases/symbols, and still cannot completely understand the meaning of a verse, then mark it as a mystery. The truth is that in prophecy God has purposely veiled some things and we may never know (at least while we live on Earth). When men come along and assign arbitrary meaning to these texts, we may have more warm fuzzy feelings, but it does not help lead us to the real truth. Either the text says it or it doesn't. Now, yes, leaving mysteries can seem unsettling, and you may even feel like you are not very smart, but be encouraged by this: Even Martin Luther, the father of the Protestant movement, who was well-studied in God's Word, said there were certain verses in the Bible he could not fully understand. He never did figure them out, even when discussing them with other very learned scholars. So, you know what he did? He admitted he did not know and left the mystery in God's hands.

The Most Misunderstood Book

If the book of Revelation was a living organism, it would surely die from inflammation. Its existence and content has been poked, prodded, and injected with all kind of foreign matter. It has been poisoned, flipped inside out, stretched beyond the breaking point, and used in ways it was never intended. So, as I said, if it was a living organism, it would likely be dead. This begs questions that ask, why? Why take a book that was meant for encouragement and create horror stories that breed fear and confusion? Revelation was written to believers, and it is a message that says God is going to take care of believers and protect them, and that he is going to seek revenge on those who have hurt the believers. God also promised a bright future for the church and eventually an eternal home for them. Does this sound like any movie you have heard about end-times? I see many end-times movies that focus on everything but the core message of Revelation.

Having studied Revelation using the RID method, I have a clearer idea about the purpose of the book, but since you may have never seen it this way, I could take the position of many eschatologists and say, before you read Revelation, keep in mind that it is XXXX. Hmm. That would be wrong. What you need to do is apply all the rules of RID. You must start at the very beginning and consider everything that is said. And, before you read the first word you must consider this: Do not take anything I have said as the right view. Do not consider any other view you have ever heard or seen in a movie. Shelf every idea that is associated with end-times or prophecy. For once in your life, read Revelation to see what the writer actually said – and what he did not say. Diligently do a Fresh Read. Read it as if you had never seen it before. If you find odd phrasing or symbols (you will find a lot), then take the time to search the Bible to see where these terms were used before. You will find many of the things in Revelation, in the Old Testament. You will be surprised at how grounded these odd symbols and phrases are when compared to texts that believers of John's time probably already knew. It was likely the people receiving the letter (Revelation) knew a lot more about what John was talking about, than you or I. Finally, for the things you cannot easily figure out, leave them as mysteries. Do not play God and start assigning possible meanings. If we assign parallels and symbolic connections, we will be as guilty as those who fabricate their own fancifully false doctrines.

Here is a truth about symbolic or riddle-oriented prophecies: Most people can take a symbol or poetic phrase and connect it with an idea. If a prophecy contains a trumpet, I can take any Bible text that includes a trumpet and say, aha, this is the meaning. I can also take a general principle or doctrine of God's Word, and claim that this prophecy is illustrating that. Because I can creatively connect an event or symbol to a parallel idea (or what I might say is parallel), does not mean that was the writer's intention. The writer very well may have meant for what is written on the page to be what was intended, and nothing more. When we start making our own parallels, using various prophecy pieces, we can actually "rewrite" the Bible. And, guess what? Our own re-written Bible is no longer the Word of God. It is our imagination, filled with cleverly created theories. Thou shalt not go there.

Be Prepared

At some point in your life, you are going to be involved in a debate about the Bible. Whether you have a good knowledge of the scripture or have just remembered a few pieces of text, you will still find yourself attempting to defend your faith. So, whether you seek debate or not, you will get it. The question remains: How prepared are you to truly defend your faith? If you recite a text you remember from the Bible, can you find that text? What if the person you are debating says, they do not believe that is in the Bible and asks you to show him where the Bible says that? Now, do not feel bad. Many people cannot accurately remember chapter and verse numbers, but with a smart phone at hand, you should be able to do a scripture search and have the information in about 2 minutes. However, if you have remembered the text wrongly, you may never find it. If you have ideas about scriptures, but cannot remember what the verses say, you are sunk. You probably will not find the text. I hear many Christians say things they have heard or seen in a meme, and they are a shortened and twisted form of a Bible verse. For example, I hear Christians often say: God won't give you more than you can handle. But, if you look this up, you may never find it. The Bible verse this is taken from, actually says this:

> **1 Corinthians 10:13 No temptation has overtaken you except what is common to mankind. And God is faithful; he will not let you be tempted beyond what you can bear.**

**But when you are tempted, he will also
provide a way out so that you can endure it.**

So, does this verse say that God will not give you more than you can handle? Hmm. It seems to say that God will not let you be "tempted" in a way that is beyond your abilities – and these abilities include a divinely provided escape route. So, if some difficult situation comes along in life, let's say a death in the family, does this verse cover that situation? No. I doubt that any good Bible teacher would say that the death of a loved one qualifies as a temptation. There may be some associated temptations that are just part of our everyday life, but the situation is not a temptation. In light of this, when a person is overcome by grief, it would be inappropriate to comfort them by saying, God will not give you more than you can handle. For goodness sake, folks. This is not helpful. Even Jesus cried when his friend died, and this was when Jesus knew his friend would be alive again that same day. If a person is grieving, the kind and Christian thing to do is to grieve with them and understand that it may very well be more than they can handle. Be the support person that helps them handle it.

Another famous misquoted idea is that money is the root of all evil. Let's look at the real verse:

**1 Timothy 6:10 For the love of money is a
root of all kinds of evil. Some people, eager
for money, have wandered from the faith and
pierced themselves with many griefs.**

Here we see that it is the love of money that is the problem, not the money itself. And, it is not "the root of evil", it is "a root of all kinds of evil." This means there are likely other roots to these evils, thus there are more paths to evil than money and they all need to be marked as trouble.

Perhaps you can see by these examples that just remembering ideas or pieces of verses may not get you very far in defending your faith or defending the Bible. Thus, you need to be prepared. How do people prepare for anything? How do you prepare for a test in school? You have to study. Now, you might say that you are not taking a test when it comes to defending your faith, but is this true? Is it not true that a person who questions you about your faith is testing your beliefs and the doctrines that support them? Isn't your belief on trial? Isn't the Bible on trial? I would say that many times they are. You will be questioned just like an oral exam. You will be put on the spot and how you answer the questions will be graded by the one asking the questions. You will pass or fail, not in the eyes of God, but in the heart of the one who is questioning your faith. So, will you give a good account of yourself and your beliefs, or not?

Here is the final question: If, when asked about your faith, you stumble and give some pat answers that you may have heard at church, then do you believe what you are saying? I mean, honestly and truthfully, do you believe there is a real God, and that his son is Jesus, sent to die for your sins? Do you really and truly believe there is a life after this one? Do you believe God wants to be actively involved in your life and has planned things for you to do? These are critical questions, and if you do believe them, you need to know why you believe them. What authority gave you this knowledge? Your preacher or God's Word? They are not the same. People can be wrong. God is not. If your faith is firm, it is because you have a wide and solid foundation. This is the kind of foundation that is not easily shaken. A shallow and small foundation can more easily be shaken, and sometimes it can even be destroyed.

What if someone told you that some of the most important books were excluded from the Bible because early church leaders knew that they would show the beliefs the church leaders wanted to forward were wrong? And what if this someone, also said that more than one of these books said that Jesus had a wife and that he did not actually die? Would you believe any of what this person said? Why or why not? Do you want to know the truth? Well, here it is in a nutshell: Many of the books that seem to tell about Jesus, but are not in the Bible are called the Gnostic Gospels. Many of these books seem to have been written around 300 AD and were meant to discredit was the Apostles wrote in the first century. The authors of these books were not Christian. As far as content is concerned, one version of one of these Gnostic documents (Gospel of Thomas, I believe) claims that Jesus had a love-relationship with Mary the Magdalene, and thus was married to her. The follow-on deduction was that Jesus had children and his descendants are still here on earth. This idea played out in the movie, "The Da Vinci Code." Of course, none of this is true. There were a lot of people named Jesus in Jesus' day. There were many before him and many after him. Most of the other Jesus' had wives and families, thus lineage. One of these other Jesus' bloodlines may have been traced. We do know that up to the time of Martin Luther, the Roman Catholic Church promoted the practice of "indulgences." This meant the church encouraged people to pay the church for their freedom from sin. The church also sold relics, like pieces of the cross, nails, or bones of the saints. Many of these were fakes of course, but people felt they needed them. The church told people that the purchase of these relics would help reduce time spent in purgatory after death. It was mostly just another way for the church to raise money. Martin Luther saw this fraud and duplicity and sharply disagreed. Eventually, he was no longer part of the Catholic Church and became the founder of the Protestants. These are important things to know and easily researched on the internet.

We need to know our Bible, well. Well, enough to know that it does not say Jesus was married or had children. In fact, it says he had no blood offspring. It is also helpful to know some of the sources of false information, and why they are not reliable. So, study and knowledge are important, when defending your faith. Grab the RID rules and read, read, read.

Arrogance: A Deadly Trap

To give you an idea of what arrogance is, let me share some of its synonyms:

> **haughtiness · conceit · hubris · self-importance · egotism · sense of superiority · pomposity · high-handedness · swagger · boasting · bluster · condescension · disdain · contempt · pride · vanity · immodesty · loftiness · lordliness · snobbishness · snobbery · smugness · pretension · pretentiousness · affectation · scorn · mocking · sneering · scoffing · presumption · insolence**

See anything in there you want to be? Hmm. How about seeing anything in there that you have been? Another hmm. Okay, I have been guilty of most of these at one time or another, especially if I was very angry, or if I felt I was being attacked personally. But, was it justified? I think asking the person who was receiving the brunt of these attitudes would be the best judge. My wife? My colleagues? Hmm. I will give you their phone numbers so you can ask them (just kidding).

There are many times in life when we get very angry. Some of these times may be justified, some not. Mostly it seems that people's anger is rooted in self-centered agendas. The point I am trying to make here is that we have emotions and it is human to have them. We have a wide variety of emotions and many of them are just fine. They fit with what we are feeling and thinking at the time. Right or wrong, they are there. What is kind of weird is that we can feel very strongly about something, yet if something else comes along that pulls us in another direction, we can put that emotion aside for the sake of the situation. I think everyone has experienced being very angry and arguing or even yelling, then the phone rings. When you answer, you often put on your sweet friendly voice and act like everything is wonderful. What happens when the call is over a few minutes later? Do you resume the same anger level? Usually not - at least not right away. So, can we control our anger? Yes, we can. We just get caught up, energetically, in a "cause," and feel like we need to defend that cause to death.

We have our "good and polite" mannerisms and we have our "warring and defensive" mannerisms. We choose which ones we will use in different circumstances. So, the question here is, what mannerism do you choose, when defending your faith? Does your mannerism include bringing out all your "guns," so you can prove the other guy wrong? Hmm. Will this win him to Christ? Probably not. Defending your faith is about winning someone to your thinking. It is about persuasion, not about winning a war. Perhaps the very definition of Apologetics is misleading. If we start with "defense," how will we ever leave that position? We are not defending, as much as presenting a factual case for why something that is, is. Our truth is verifiable and quite plain. We do not need to defend the fact that it is real, because it already is. We need to shift our focus and our position. If we consider we are in some kind of courtroom, what position are we in? Are we the judge? Certainly not. Are we the prosecuting attorney? Heaven forbid. Are we, then the defense attorney? Well, many scholars and apologists, may think so. Some arguments can be made for us being the defenders, but let me suggest another position. I see scripture casting believers in the role of "witness." If this is true, then we are not the defenders, we are the witnesses. We are not the ones who are on trial – Jesus is. We are witnesses of who he is and what he has done for us. We tell about our relationship with him and his good character. We testify of his reliable and loving nature, and his noble intentions. In this process, we are probed, and our testimony is questioned for reliability and accuracy, but what is being determined is what Christ has done and is doing. It is not about you, so don't be trapped into thinking or acting like it is. Even if your character is attacked, it is because of a desire to vet the veracity of Jesus.

A witness for Christ should never take on any of the things that are in the synonym list. When we are telling about Jesus and what the Bible says about him, we give our information with gentleness and respect. We try to bring honor to him. Acting ugly does not bring him honor. Frankly, it does not bring us any honor, either. You can be right and even win an argument, yet lose a person's respect. If they do not respect you, they will not follow you or anything you present. They may leave you, admitting you are right, yet see you as an enemy. How can an enemy lead you anywhere, much less to Christ?

Win souls, not arguments.

Best Way to Read the Bible

There are many ways to just read the Bible, and no set or advertised way is better than another. Each person should read the Bible the way that suits them best. You need to consider your lifestyle, available time periods, and your ability to be alone with God while you are reading.

<u>In a Year?</u>

One method of Bible reading is to read the whole Bible in a year. There are charts to help you do this, and even Bibles specifically laid out in daily reading portions. If you find this rewarding, or just do not know what all the books of the Bible say, then please try this out, at least once. It is not hard. You can do it with only about 10 minutes of reading per day. It is good for an overview of the Bible's content, but unless you have very good retention, you will probably end up losing half or more of what you read. Another thing to think about is that because this is a regimented course if you fall behind, you may need to spend some serious time catching up. Of course, you can always go over that year mark and skip a day, here or there. However, I think it is important to consider that when you skip some days, you can get out of the habit, and if you lose the pace and impetus, you may also lose interest and just drop reading altogether.

Now, if you want excellent retention and do not care about how fast you get through the Bible, as long as you do get through, then read the Bible for content, rather than for conquered real estate.

<u>One Book?</u>

If you are a rigorous and fast reader, you can read a whole Bible book each day (Jude does not count). On average, this will be about 18 chapters a day. At this pace, you would read through the whole Bible in 66 days. However, how much would you remember? Hmm. Hard to say.

Now, this is a cool goal, but again, you have to look at your lifestyle and see if this is realistic. Some "A" type personalities want to conquer the world in a day and see no reason why they cannot. Unfortunately, when they find that there are obstacles in life they cannot control, they can become impatient and just give up. This is bad. Other types of personalities will cautiously jump into a noble goal like this and end up discouraged and even guilty because they did not have the drive to continue such an arduous task. So, your work schedule, family commitments, and rest time, as well as your personality, play a part in whether this choice is right for you.

Again, the goal of reading the Bible is to take in what it says and live it. If I am reading to just put pages behind me, then my reading may be more for pride than Spiritual benefit.

A Chapter Each Day?

Reading only a chapter a day may fit better with your lifestyle and this is absolutely okay. It will take much longer to get through the Bible, of course, but it is a good idea.

When I was about 12 years old, I committed to reading one chapter every night, after I hopped in bed. I think it set up something very valuable in my life, and I still read the Bible every night (unless external issues prevent it) when I go to bed. One good aspect about reading in this way is that it tends to embed thoughts in my head that are not mixed with all my daily responsibilities.

A Better Way

There should be a time in your day when you put away deep Bible study, and just read for personal time with God. It nourishes your soul and it helps keep you in a closer relationship with God and his son. To help you see how this is important, let me share something with you.

When I was about 25 years old, God impressed me with something strong and clear. He said, "I want to talk to you." Up to that point in my life, I thought only super-spiritual people heard from God, and everyone else had to go by signs, but this message to me was different and powerful. It was not just a thought or impression. This word came with a very powerful presence of God. The kind that you feel when God is there in a church service and you can feel and know it is him. At about this same time, I started reading my Bible in the early morning. I would grab some food, and sit down with my Bible. I would pray and ask God to show me what I needed to know that day, then I would read the Bible and just listen with my spirit. Do you know what happened? I heard. Nearly every day God spoke to me about my life, and what I needed to do. He encouraged me and showed me more of his love. This transformed my life. So, what was a key element in this life-transforming scenario? Certainly prayer and an open heart, but it was married with a method of reading God's Word that was different from what I had done before.

I read to hear God speak to me.

The wonderful and important thing is that when I received that special word from him, it was like gold to me. It was my special nugget for that day. This changed my life and it changed my whole concept of daily Bible reading. And, you know what? I still read the same way. At least one time each day, I look for God's direction and his presence, while reading the Bible. As a pastor, I read a lot of the Bible for other things, but this one time is special and will always be.

A Final Word

I want to leave you with some final thoughts. Complicating God's Word does not make it better. Just because a person can create complex connections between scores of verses, does not mean the idea is correct or well-founded. The best and most solid doctrines of the Bible are rooted in "teachings." These teachings come from either God himself, or someone he has appointed. In the Bible, we should be looking for significant passages where an idea is presented and explained. The idea will be clear and so will how the idea is elaborated. For instance, when Jesus taught the multitudes, he would often talk about an idea, then give word illustrations of that idea. This is teaching about a subject. So, what is not teaching on a subject? Well, let me try to make this clear: If, for example, the Apostle Paul is writing to one of the churches, and he is obviously answering a question or issue of the church, then in the middle of his answer he inserts a couple of sentences that reference something related, but different, those inserted sentences are not complete teaching on that subject. What Paul is doing is using an example of something else to support what he is trying to teach. The example is not being taught, the idea he is addressing is what he is teaching. Paul may have a whole Bible page dedicated to teaching about the issue that came up in the church, then insert just a verse or two, to show how his answer is supported by other ideas. This has become problematic, especially in Eschatology, because these inserted verses have often become the very foundation for end-times theories. And, why would we not want to use these inserted verses as a base for additional doctrine? Because, again, Paul is not actually teaching on it. The inserted thoughts are not explained or detailed. Thus, theorizers can take a few words and build all kinds of elaborate doctrines. Beware of this kind of Eschatology. It does not have a solid base. It can turn out to be a cream-puff doctrine that sounds exciting but has no solid and reliable core.

What we should be looking for, are whole passages or at least complete paragraphs in the Bible, where the speaker is talking about one subject, and that subject is obvious. This is the very essence of not manipulating scripture. We want the plain, in-your-face, glaring, and obvious truth. These support a defense of our faith in a way that is formidable. They have a broad and solid base that an opponent can find hard to wriggle out of. These are the rocks we can stand on that are immovable. They stand the test of time and countless arguments. Thus, our faith stands firm, because it is built on these doctrinal rocks.

One of the ways we can build or identify these "faith rocks" is by using the RID rules. It is not the only good study rule system, but it is likely the most simple - while still being effective. RID allows us to first get just what is on the Bible page and consider the text on its own merit. It also offers a slightly deeper look, when the words on the page sound odd (compared to our everyday language). And, in the end, if we cannot easily decipher it without creating theories, then we can accept the mystery as something that may have purposely been veiled. At this point, we let God be God and we do not try to insert meaning that God never said. Once this whole cycle of RID thought and practice is complete, you should be able to properly identify the correct Biblical doctrines. There should be no extra varnish or decorations added to the text, and there should be no surgery to remove unwanted text. Just the facts.

To keep Bible study and our relation with Jesus in proper balance, it is also very important that we take special time to just connect with our Savior. If we sit down with the Bible and simply ask Jesus to show us what we need, today, he will begin to show us how the Bible text relates to our lives. God can give you daily insight that will help you with what is currently going on in your life. This is the Spiritual "gold" that often carries us through tough times and helps us know Jesus better.

So, I encourage you to take time away from cross-references, expository, interlinears, and concordances. Just read and listen to what God speaks to you. It can give you a whole new outlook on life. And, please, do not make this time just the same old thing you do. Each time can be special and it can be different. The place is not so important, as long as it has no other distractions. Be selfish with this time, and do not let anything rob you or God of your precious time together. This time can be extended or it can be quite short. It is not about the time, as much as fully getting what God is trying to tell you - then taking time to think about it and letting it sink in - then taking that with you, all day - and living it.

<u>My Hope</u>

I hope and pray that you found some useful things in this book. Clarity of scripture is important and this is what we are striving for. This is what we encourage our Christian brothers and sisters to do, also. It is time we filter out the doctrinal junk that is so pervasive in the Christian church. It is time, we seek truth with more vigor. It is time we speak up and stop allowing the bullies to tell everyone they must believe traditions, no matter how poorly they are supported in scripture. This kind of bullying is what the Catholic Church did for centuries, and why we Protestants rebelled. I think it is time for a little rebellion in the church - not against the authority of leadership, but against unsupported doctrines.

Prove it or shelf it!

Make your teachers prove what they teach, and make them prove it with actual Biblical teachings, not inserted phrases that are not fully explained. Ask your teachers probing questions, and drive them back to the Word for answers, over and over again. Make them have to do research they have never done before. Try hard to leave the learned rhetoric and seek out what the Bible says - without manipulation. Your teachers may get frustrated, but if they are good teachers, they will want to know the "why" also. They will want to know the reasons a doctrine uses verses that are out of context. They will begin to see that when these badly used verses are removed from supporting a doctrine, there remains little to hold it up. A doctrine should not be maintained if the things that hold it up are false. And, many times (not always) verses that are taken out of context are "false," in their meaning. Why? Again, it is because a single verse or phrase can be convoluted and flipped upside down in an attempt to convince people who are not reading the Bible. Several doctrines and traditions we currently have in the church world are built on shaky and/or false ground. However, when we just read what is on the Bible page (in context) and do not twist it, we can more easily see the bald-faced truth. So …

Go forth and RID the world of false doctrine!

www.ingramcontent.com/pod-product-compliance
Lightning Source LLC
Chambersburg PA
CBHW071403150726
48000CB00001B/138